CLOUDS OF DECEIT

The Deadly Legacy
of Britain's Bomb Tests

by
JOAN SMITH

faber and faber

LONDON · BOSTON

First published in 1985
by Faber and Faber Limited
3 Queen Square London WC1N 3AU

Photoset and printed in Great Britain by
Redwood Burn Limited, Trowbridge, Wiltshire
All rights reserved

British Library Cataloguing in Publication Data

Smith, Joan
Clouds of deceit : the deadly legacy of
Britain's bomb tests.
1. Atomic bomb—Great Britain—Testing—
Hygienic aspects—History
I. Title
358'.39   UG1282.A8

ISBN 0–571–13628–1
ISBN 0–571–13629–X Pbk

CONTENTS

This book is dedicated to the victims
of nuclear testing all over the world

INTRODUCTION

I was born into the nuclear age: the first British atom bomb had been tested at an island off Western Australia ten months before. I can just remember seeing newsreel film of H-bomb tests when my mother took me to the cinema for the first time at the age of four or five. The mushroom cloud, familiar to me from those newsreels and from the newspapers read by my parents, symbolized the cold-war atmosphere in which I grew up.

Over the years, the image faded and lost much of its power. Until the end of 1982, I had not given the bomb tests a moment's thought for a very long time. I had been a journalist on the *Sunday Times* for three years, while acting as occasional adviser to a television company which made current affairs films for Channel Four. At the end of 1982, the company told me about a film they were working on about the British atom bomb tests in the 1950s. It consisted largely of footage bought in from Australia, where men who took part in the tests were already campaigning for compensation for ill-health which, they said, was caused by the tests.

I saw a preview of the film in January 1983 and wrote an article about it in the *Sunday Times*. The BBC's *Nationwide* had just made some programmes about the health of veterans of Britain's hydrogen bomb tests at Christmas Island and in the face of this publicity the government moved into action, of a sort – it announced it would commission a survey of the health of men who participated in all the British tests.

The story seemed exactly the kind of investigative journalism the *Sunday Times* should take up. Prima facie, the men appeared to be the unwitting victims of a powerful and monolithic entity. The letters I received from veterans, and the tough line taken by the Ministry of Defence, suggested they would have a long struggle ahead in their search for answers from the government. Their case could have been helped immeasurably by the kind of campaigning and investigative journalism on which the paper had built its reputation in the 1960s and 1970s, under Harold Evans.

Unfortunately, the *Sunday Times* had undergone radical changes since those days. The major one was, of course, the sale of the paper in 1981 by the Thomson Organisation to Rupert Murdoch. At first, I managed to secure reasonable coverage for the veterans' claims in spite of the new regime: many of the old staff remained and maintained their commitment to investigative journalism. On 16 January 1983, I wrote the main feature in that week's paper; it was headlined 'A-BOMB TESTS: WILL JUSTICE BE DONE?'

It included further stories of lax safety precautions and cited evidence from the US which showed that an atom bomb test in Nevada in the 1950s appeared to have caused leukaemia in American servicemen. It also identified a major obstacle in the veterans' path: the Crown Proceedings Act 1947, which denies servicemen compensation for injuries sustained during their service.

In the spring of 1983, I tried to persuade the *Sunday Times* to launch an *Insight*-style investigation into the claims of the veterans. I received support for this idea from Dr Alice Stewart, of Birmingham University, who was already looking at the health of one group of veterans, those who had been at Christmas Island, and from the then editor of *Insight*, Christopher Hird. But the attitude of other executives was ambivalent. The paper was feeling the cash restraints imposed by the Murdoch management and was reluctant to commit itself to time-consuming journalism of this sort; its preference for the big, easy story became apparent only months later when it embroiled itself in the Hitler diaries fiasco.

Another problem was the temperament of Frank Giles, who had succeeded Harry Evans as editor in 1981. Unfortunately, his upper-middle-class punctiliousness, combined with his early career in the diplomatic corps, had given him a distaste for Evans-style investigative journalism. He once described the term to me as 'a tautology', on the grounds that journalism was *ipso facto* investigative; he was apparently unaware that this notion is daily dispelled by the content of newspapers like the *Sun*. He vetoed the project.

I did what I could within the limited resources of the newsroom budget, and in between the many other calls on my time made by the newsdesk. This situation continued through most of 1983. By keeping in touch with the veterans, and scientists who worked in the field of low-level radiation – and with the enthusiastic help of the newsroom researcher, Carol Baker – I managed to produce a number of stories about the bomb tests.

In October 1983, a new editor took over and my problems increased. The change, which happened very quickly, meant that the executives' previous argument that the paper could not really afford to do old-fashioned investigative journalism turned into outright prohibition. The political climate had altered.

In that month, for the first time in my career at the *Sunday Times*, a story I had written was kept out of the paper on political grounds: its subject was CND. Sadly, I was not the only journalist to suffer from political interference. By January 1984, many of the journalistic staff were demoralized. Some had left, others had been sacked.

At the end of the month, I was summoned to an interview with one of the paper's executives. He told me that the new editor, Andrew Neil, felt I had 'got into a rut' on nuclear stories. It was a curious reversal of the old practice at the paper, under which reporters were encouraged to gain expertise in particular fields which interested them.

The message was clear: stories that might damage the nuclear industry were no longer welcome at the *Sunday Times*. Six weeks later, I obtained a damaging document about the bomb tests which had been released to the Public Records Office at Kew by the government. The newsdesk was clearly reluctant to run the story. In the end, it appeared on an inside page, inconspicuously sited below the fold. The ruse failed to work as the following day Australian newspapers picked up the story and blazed it across their front pages. The chaos reigning at the *Sunday Times* was amply demonstrated later in the same week when I was asked to follow up a report that an inquiry had been set up in Australia as a result of my tucked-away revelation. On 31 March 1984, I left the paper and decided to write this book.

The story of the British nuclear tests has unfolded slowly, and is not yet finished. My purpose in writing this book has been twofold. I wanted to tell, at length, enough of the tale to demonstrate that the British government has a substantial case to answer. I also wanted to show that the bomb tests are not part of the past, as I believed only two-and-a-half years ago.

They remain with us in the shape of the victims: the British and Australian servicemen and civilians who, I believe, have become ill and even died because of the tests; and the aborigines, many of whom were damaged by radiation and whose traditional homelands have been turned into a radioactive wasteland.

The tests are still with us in another sense as well: they have continued without a break to the present day. Britain now tests nuclear weapons underground in Nevada, as does the US; radiation regularly escapes and irradiates further the unfortunate people who live near the testing site. Russia has similarly continued testing.

The tests are a hidden testimony to the continued existence of the cold war. In the forty years since the end of the Second World War, it has never gone away – it has merely submerged from our consciousness from time to time. We will know that the major powers are serious about drawing back from the threshold of world war only when they take the first step of putting an end to nuclear weapons tests.

My task in writing this book was made much easier by the decision of the Australian government to set up a Royal Commission to examine allegations about the British tests. I have drawn heavily on the evidence of witnesses who appeared before it, and documents released to it by the British government. While the analysis and views expressed in this book are mine alone, I received invaluable assistance while researching it from the following people: Ken McGinley and Michael Doyle, of the British Nuclear Tests Veterans' Association; Peter McClellan, the barrister who assisted the Australian Royal Commission; Andrew Collett, the barrister who represented the aborigines; and Greenpeace. Margaret Gowing's three-volume history of the early days of Britain's nuclear programme was an excellent guide to the events leading up to the bomb tests. Patrick Green's thesis on the low-level radiation controversy provided a comprehensive and thoughtful view of the issue.

Vital additional research was carried out by Carol Baker in London, and by Robert Milliken in London and Sydney. Support and helpful suggestions came from Jennifer Benjamin, Anita Bennett, Barbara Crossley, Linda Lewis, Bruce Palling, John Shirley, Giles Stacey and Gill Williams. I am grateful to my agent, Sara Drake, and my editor for their help and enthusiasm. Francis Wheen suggested the project and provided a constant and reassuring presence during the writing of it; to him I owe a debt I hope to repay with love.

Joan Smith
London, April 1985

British Nuclear Weapons Tests in Australia and the South Pacific

Operation	Date	Size	Location	Name
Hurricane	3.10.52	25 kilotons†	Monte Bello Islands	
Totem	14.10.53	10 kilotons	Emu Field, S. Australia	
	26.10.53	8 kilotons	ditto	
Mosaic	16.5.56	15 kilotons	Monte Bello Islands	
	19.6.56	98 kilotons	ditto	
Buffalo	27.9.56	15 kilotons	Maralinga, S. Australia	*One Tree*
	4.10.56	1.5 kilotons	ditto	*Marcoo*
	11.10.56	3 kilotons	ditto	*Kite*
	21.10.56	10 kilotons	ditto	*Breakaway*
Antler	14.9.57	1 kiloton	ditto	*Tadje*
	25.9.57	6 kilotons	ditto	*Biak*
	9.10.57	25 kilotons	ditto	*Taranaki*
Grapple	15.5.57	megaton range*	Malden Island, S. Pacific	
	31.5.57	ditto	ditto	
	19.6.57	ditto	ditto	
Grapple X	8.11.57	megaton range	Christmas Island, S. Pacific	
Grapple Y	28.4.58	ditto	ditto	
Grapple Z	22.8.58	kiloton range	ditto	
	2.9.58	megaton range	ditto	
	11.9.58	ditto	ditto	
	23.9.58	kiloton range	ditto	

† The government has released exact figures showing the yield of the atom bomb tests which took place in Australia. A kiloton bomb is equal to 1,000 tons of conventional explosive, such as TNT.

* The government has not released the yields of the hydrogen and atom bombs tested in the South Pacific. A megaton is the equivalent to one million tons of TNT. Some of the British H-bombs were as large as 10 million tons of TNT.

CHAPTER ONE

'What the bloody hell is going on?'

Message from the acting prime minister
of Australia, 19 June 1956, as a
radioactive cloud drifted over the mainland

Christmas Island is the largest coral atoll in the Pacific Ocean. It lies just north of the equator, three-and-a-half thousand nautical miles to the north-east of Sydney. It is also the place where, between November 1957 and September 1958, Britain exploded six nuclear weapons, including four hydrogen bombs. British servicemen who witnessed the bomb tests were told that they would remember the experience for the rest of their lives.

One of those men was Ken McGinley, a young Scottish sapper in the Royal Engineers. McGinley was just 19 years old when he left Southampton on New Year's Eve 1957 on board the troop ship *Dunera*, bound for the Pacific Ocean. 'Our sergeant only told us what we were going to see when we were three weeks out,' McGinley recalled nearly thirty years later. 'Even then, we were only told we were going to witness bombs going off – not nuclear bombs, not atomic bombs, just bombs. I hadn't heard anything about bomb tests, I hadn't even heard of Hiroshima and Nagasaki. What boy or girl of nineteen had? We weren't interested in bombs.'

Nevertheless, by the time McGinley left Christmas Island a full twelve months later, he had been lined up on a beach on five separate occasions to witness bomb tests. He had seen dozens of men around him suffer violent stomach upsets from shock, had been given the gruesome task of picking up the corpses of burned and blinded birds for dumping at sea, and he had suffered blisters on his face and chest. The blisters, which appeared four days after McGinley's first test, a hydrogen bomb on 28 April 1958, were only the harbinger of a catalogue of ill health which led to his being pensioned off from the service at the end of 1959. At the age of only 21, McGinley found himself out of the army and in possession of a 30 per cent disability pension. He was suffering from blackouts and a duodenal ulcer. His GP, who examined him just before he left the army, told him: 'You will regret for the rest of your life that you were at Christmas Island.' But McGinley's other medical problem was not to become apparent for some years.

In 1960, McGinley got married. He and his wife, Alice, desperately wanted a child. Both come from large families, a tradition which has been carried on by McGinley's five brothers and sisters who have twenty-four children between them. His wife's three sisters also have numerous children. But McGinley discovered he was sterile. 'I'm 100 per cent positive it's because I was at Christmas Island,' he said. He has since found out that three other men out of the seven with whom he shared his tent have been unable to have children. Radiation is known to cause sterility.

On his return to Britain from Christmas Island, McGinley had been told not to speak to anyone about what he had seen there. It was an injunction he obeyed until November 1982, when he was told that his army pension was to be reviewed. He obtained his service medical records and discovered, to his astonishment, that they were incomplete. The blisters which appeared after the April 1958 bomb, and which were severe enough to require twelve days' treatment, were not mentioned. 'I was disgusted to find they were not complete and might even have been tampered with,' he said. He decided to break his silence and write to a Scottish newspaper, claiming his health had been damaged by the tests. Six months later, he became chairman of the newly-formed British Nuclear Tests Veterans' Association.

McGinley runs the association from his guest house at East Bay, Dunoon. He is a small, wiry man with a gentle Scottish accent. Just over two years since it was set up, the association has 1,300 members and takes up a good deal of Ken McGinley's energy. 'I could spend twenty-four hours a day and still not have enough time,' he observed wryly. But his memories of events at Christmas Island remain undimmed and he is eager to establish the truth of what happened not just for himself but for all the others who took part – and their widows.

'We arrived at Christmas Island very early one morning in February 1958,' he recalled. 'It was gorgeous. What I noticed about it first of all was the barrier reef, you saw the water breaking against it all the time. It was more or less a flat island with no vegetation other than coconuts. There wasn't much animal life, just rats and crabs, but there were lots of birds. They were funny-looking birds, we used to call them Grapple birds after the name of the Operation. After the April 28 bomb, one of my jobs was to lift them up and put them on a landing craft to be taken out to sea. Some of them were still alive but they were blind, their eyes had been burned out.'

When McGinley arrived at the island, the islanders, who originated from what were then called the Gilbert and Ellice Islands, lived in a village near to one of the military camps. 'I couldn't say how many of them there were,' said McGinley, 'but two or three of the men worked with us in the camp. They were very friendly people. They were taken away from the island the day before each explosion. I herded them on to the ship. They were taken below deck and shown cartoon films.'

The men were told only the day before each test when it was to take place. 'All we were told to do was sit on the beach. They would start the countdown and then say "hold it, that was a dummy run". They would do that three or four times. You could be sitting on that beach in one hundred degrees for two hours. Two or three guys fainted. It was very uncomfortable. We were never given protective clothing. I remember distinctly what I wore – my jungle green hat, jacket and long trousers. We were told to cover our ears with our hands when the flash appeared.

'When the bomb went off, it was uncanny. We watched its effect on the water. It was very still and then, all of a sudden, you saw the wave coming towards you. The noise was deafening, like a thousand horses thundering towards you. The man next to me broke down and cried. A lot of men suffered from immediate diarrhoea. After each bomb, it was very noticeable on the night of the explosion that you could hardly get near the toilets. It was really, really terrible.'

Some men suffered skin burns, McGinley himself came out in blisters. There were other problems, too. 'I did notice that some men suffered psychiatric problems,' said McGinley. 'Some of the Fijians [a number of Fijian soldiers took part in the tests with the British] were sent home. Later in the series of tests, in September, it became even more noticeable. Men would do anything to get sent back to the UK. One of them set fire to the hospital tent. Discipline was terrible and all kinds of assaults took place quite regularly.'

Horrific though the actual tests were, McGinley's other vivid recollection is of the relentless boredom of life on Christmas Island. The men's diet consisted almost solely of canned food, with no fresh milk to be had except for what they got on occasional trips to Hawaii. The food was often thrown into the sand in disgust. 'We didn't realize we were going to be stuck out there for a year,' McGinley recalled. 'There was nothing to do to keep us occupied, nothing at all.'

Since he became one of the first British veterans to air his complaints publicly, McGinley has heard innumerable stories like his own from other Christmas Island veterans and those who took part in the British atom bomb tests in Australia. His mail is full of letters from veterans or their widows, some recounting their experiences for the first time, others bringing him up to date on their battles with the British government over pensions, or describing the latest developments in their illnesses. One of his most heartbreaking tasks as chairman of the association is advising the newly-bereaved widows of veterans who turn to him for advice on how to go about finding out what happened to their husbands at the tests.

In just over two years, about ninety members of the association have died. Many are relatively young men in their late forties or early fifties. Often, their widows become active members of the association in their place.

McGinley's work for the association is often harrowing, but one particular experience haunts him to this day. One evening in November 1983, he received a phone call from a man who told him starkly: 'I'm phoning on behalf of my widow.' After this unnerving opening, the man went on to explain that he was an

RAF officer, a squadron leader who had served at Christmas Island. Knowing himself to be dying from cancer, and about to go back into hospital for yet another course of treatment, he had decided to ring the association to ask for help for his wife. 'When I die, I want you to get those bastards,' he told McGinley. He died a month later. 'That's the kind of thing that makes you fight on,' McGinley told me.

Colonel Peter Lowe lives in Warminster, Wiltshire. In 1957, he was sent to Maralinga, in South Australia, to watch a series of weapon tests in order to lecture troops on the effects of nuclear weapons. He is one of the many British ex-servicemen who gave evidence in 1985 to the Australian Royal Commission investigating the British nuclear tests which took place on Australian territory. In terms of class and rank, his background and experience are utterly different from Ken McGinley's, but in many other respects the two men have much in common. Both retain vivid memories of the tests, particularly of the lax attitude to safety and, like Ken McGinley, Peter Lowe believes that the tests he attended may have caused him lasting physical damage.

Lowe travelled to Sydney in 1957 on a BOAC flight via the Far East, before going on to Maralinga. There were about 200–300 other British army personnel at Maralinga at the time, including British army observers from the UK and all overseas commands – Germany, Middle and Far East, and Africa. All administrative support was provided by the Australian Army; there were also some personnel from the New Zealand army. Lowe was stationed at '11 Mile Camp', eleven miles away from the detonation area. It was a tented camp and, according to Lowe, conditions there were 'fairly primitive'.

Although he had been told that his stay might be as short as three weeks, he soon realized that it would be longer because of the delay caused by waiting for the weather to be correct for detonation. While waiting for the weather to change, the troops were given a series of lectures about the hazards of radiation and the mechanics of the atom bomb. Lowe found the lectures given by Sir William Penney, the scientist in charge of the tests, to be 'extremely interesting and well presented', but those of the other lecturers 'tended to be too technical to understand or were badly put across'.

Penney told them that an excess of gamma radiation would be hazardous to their health, but that the organizers would ensure that there was no such excess exposure. He said that on the day after detonation, the servicemen would go into a contaminated area with full protective clothing, including a film badge, radiation monitor and gas mask. One man in each party would have a portable Geiger counter.

As part of their preparation for the explosion, Lowe and his colleagues spent the best part of three weeks 'digging in' a range of equipment – 25-pounder guns, machine guns and mortars – about two miles from ground zero (the point nearest the blast). They also erected field defences and radio aerials, and put out field telephones. The purpose of all this was to test the effects of the blast and heat on military equipment.

Lowe watched the first explosion from a hillside about five miles away from ground zero. The next day, he and the other troops went into the target area in groups of between six and eight. They were taken in a three-ton truck to the edge of the contaminated area, where they donned gas masks, boots and protective clothing, which they called 'Noddy suits'. They then walked to the place where they had left the equipment before the explosion, to measure the effects of the blast on it.

As the senior officer in his group, Lowe was issued with a hand-held Geiger counter and briefly instructed as to how it worked, and how he would know when the danger level had been reached. He was told that when the needle went near the danger level, or the clicking of the counter became too fast, they should withdraw from the contaminated area at once.

'After we left the three-ton truck, we walked towards ground zero,' he recalled. 'I cannot estimate how close to ground zero we went. We were not walking in a straight line because each of us had our own particular interest. Mine, as a gunner, was in the equipment of the Royal Artillery which I had helped to put out. We wandered around ever closer to ground zero until the Geiger counter I was holding registered what I considered a dangerous level.

18

'If the dial on the Geiger counter was a semicircle, running from 9 o'clock to 3 o'clock, and the red line was at 12 o'clock, I would estimate we withdrew after the needle had gone past 11 o'clock. The other teams withdrew at roughly the same time.' They went back to a meeting-point, from where they were taken to a decontamination camp run by the Australians.

Lowe was astonished by the insouciant attitude of the staff at the decontamination camp. 'I remember vividly a burly Australian sergeant ripping my film badge from my lapel, taking one look at it, and throwing it into a bucket. I do not remember that the film badge had any number on it. If it did, I was certainly not present when it was issued to me by number, and the number recorded. I am equally certain that no record was made of the reading by the sergeant, and that the film badge was simply consigned to a bucket like everybody else's. We then undressed and our protective clothing was taken away. I do not know what happened to it.' The men then took a shower and, after being tested with a Geiger counter, dressed in their own clothes again.

Lowe observed the second blast from the inside of a closed-down tank, which he found 'very scary indeed'. He did not know exactly how far the tank was from ground zero, but it must have been reasonably close, since the blast moved the tank about ten feet sideways. 'I was watching through a periscope, and the periscope went opaque straight away because of the sand-blasting effect, which ruined the optics.' Lowe was wearing ordinary military gear for this exercise, with no film badge. After a 'decent interval' had elapsed after the blast, he was told to evacuate the tank and return by truck to 11 Mile Camp.

At the time, Peter Lowe was not aware that his exposure might have affected his health. It was not until 1969, when he was British military attaché in Washington DC, that his illness began. He seemed to have gastric problems, but all the medical tests he was given proved negative. When he returned from Washington he went to the Royal Hospital in Millbank, London. He told the doctors there that he didn't feel well, but was simply told 'not to make a fuss'.

In 1972, when he was military adviser to the British High Commission in Canberra, he had an internal haemorrhage. The doctor who examined him said that he had either a duodenal ulcer or cancer. Lowe's tour of duty in Australia was cut short.

In 1973, when he had returned from Australia, Lowe went to a Harley Street specialist, who confirmed that he had a duodenal ulcer. Lowe persuaded him to operate to remove it. During the course of the operation, at the King Edward VII Hospital for Officers, the surgeon discovered that Lowe had a stomach tumour and immediately removed his whole stomach. Since then, Lowe has had no recurrence of his problem, but he is reviewed by the senior consultant at the Royal Marsden Hospital every six months.

The Ministry of Defence denied any liability for Lowe's trouble. It even went so far as to tell the officers' association, which was conducting Lowe's application for a pension, that he was not present at the second explosion. 'I am absolutely certain that I was,' Lowe retorted, 'and have a very vivid recollection of being stationed in the tank. I know that someone went sick at the last moment, and I took his place, and I believe that army records were never adjusted to take account of this.'

Colin Campbell was also sent to Maralinga. 'I did not volunteer – they did not ask for any volunteers at my station,' he told the Royal Commission. He was posted to Australia in 1956, at the age of 21. At the time, he was a senior aircraftsman stationed at RAF Edzell, in Scotland.

Campbell was told that he had been posted to Australia for 'general duties'. Before he left, he was given a full positive vetting, so he realised that the work was, as he put it, 'of a secret nature'. But beyond that he was kept in total ignorance. He knew nothing about Maralinga or atom bomb tests. He was given no warnings or lectures about radiation or other effects of the tests.

'When we arrived at Maralinga', he recalled, 'the construction work had been finished. All three Australian services were there. I was in the Maralinga village camp. I remember the permanent buildings were the mess hall, cook houses, offices and station HQ. There were also mechanical workshops and a cinema.'

Campbell was on driving duties around the camp until the tests began. By the time the first detonation was due to take place, everyone knew why they were there, but there were still no lectures on the effects of radiation. On 1 August 1956, Campbell was promoted to corporal. For all the tests except one, Campbell took part in parades on the airfield. For one of them, however, he was the driver of a Leyland 2,500-gallon fuel tanker, known as a Bowser. This is how he described the experience:

'A Canberra aircraft which had flown through the atomic cloud landed to refuel. I drove the Bowser out to it and an aircraft handler connected the open-line fuel supply to the aircraft. I was wearing a pair of denim overalls and ordinary shoes. I had no gloves, no head cover, and while I may possibly have had a canvas face mask, like that of a surgeon, I had no eye covering.

'I parked the Bowser between ten and fifteen feet from the aircraft while the refuelling took place. I stood at the rear of the Bowser, by the pumping controls. While I was doing this, I saw a man with a long probe, which he inserted into the sampling pod on the starboard wingtip, and pulled out the filter, which he put into a box. He was wearing the same as me. I know this, because if he had been wearing protective clothing and I wasn't, I would have wondered why. When I had finished refuelling, I drove the Bowser back to the bulk depot to refill it. After this, I went through the decontamination unit, where I showered and was then tested with a Geiger counter. I was said to be acceptably clean externally.

'I remember that the decontamination personnel used to tease the men by holding up a fluorescent watch near the counter, making it sound off, and then insisting that the personnel went through the showers again.'

In 1968, Campbell started to suffer from pulmonary fibrosis. According to Campbell, a doctor told him that it could have been caused by exposure to radiation. He told the Royal Commission that he had arranged to have a whole body scan at Harwell, but that this had then been refused on the grounds that staff there could not give him any result which could be used in proceedings against the government.

Britain's very first atom bomb was detonated on board HMS *Plym* in the Monte Bello Islands, off the west coast of Australia, on 3 October 1952. The ship was vaporized in the blast. Graham Mabbutt, who is now a policeman in Devon, was an acting petty officer on HMS *Zeebrugge* at the time of the blast. Although Mabbutt never went ashore, he watched the explosion from the deck of his ship – and had a hair-raising experience on the journey home.

On the voyage out, however, Mabbutt and his colleagues were happily ignorant of the dangers to which they would be exposed. At the time his ship left England, the crew knew only that they were going on a top-secret mission. Once they had set sail for Australia, they were officially told that they were to witness the explosion of the first British atom bomb. During the voyage to Australia, the men were given just two short lectures, delivered by two scientists who had joined the boat at Southampton. These lectures, Mabbutt recalled, were largely devoted to an explanation of the nature of nuclear fission, rather than radiation and its health hazards. The men were told that they would wear a film badge around their waist from the time of the explosion onwards, but no one bothered to explain to them how the badge worked or how it was read.

When the ship reached the Monte Bello Islands, it was positioned between twelve and fifteen miles away from the lagoon where the bomb was to be exploded. The crew were gathered on the upper deck to witness the explosion. Soon afterwards, a helicopter from HMS *Campania* arrived with canisters of radioactive samples, which were winched down on to the *Zeebrugge*'s upper deck. Scientists then carried the canisters, which were not all that bulky, down to the laboratory on board the ship. According to Mabbutt, a large number of these canisters arrived in the hours immediately after the explosion. Over the next few days, there were further drops of canisters from helicopters.

This was not the only radioactive material which was being brought on to HMS *Zeebrugge*. The Royal Marines who were stationed on the ship were going ashore in landing and assault craft to pick up samples from 'dirty areas'; these were taken to the ship's lab for testing. When the Marines talked about their work, Mabbutt recalled, 'they told me they would sometimes have their radiation instruments going off the scale, because they were too close to the dirty area, and had to retreat as fast as possible'.

Only a small proportion of the radioactive samples which came aboard was actually kept for laboratory analysis. The rest had to be disposed of – overboard. 'I was told we were going to a particularly deep part of the ocean to do this,' Mabbutt recalled. 'The waste matter was in steel drums. I was in charge of winching the drums out of the tank space from the laboratory on to the upper deck, and then overboard. There were twenty to thirty drums in all, and to my certain knowledge six to eight of them were seeping badly. There was a problem in that the davit would not swing properly because it was too small, and the drum would catch in the scuppers. I then had to step forward and manually shove the drum clear of the ship's side. I did this because I was in charge of the operation.

'I remember getting splashed over the arms and legs by the seeping liquids from these drums. I can clearly remember a scientist who was observing these operations saying, when he saw me being splashed, "One day you may live to regret that." This raised a laugh among the ratings present, as it was taken to mean that it might affect my ability to have children. Some of the drums were leaking so badly that the liquid was draining into the scuppers.'

There was always a scientist present when the drums went overboard, but when he observed the leaking he simply shrugged his shoulders, according to Mabbutt. Two or three of the drums failed to sink; again the scientist shrugged his shoulders. While this operation went on, the men were bare-armed, with sleeves rolled up.

Some of the landing and assault craft were too radioactive to be brought back to England, but others did make the journey – with consequences that gave Graham Mabbutt a nasty fright. 'When we arrived back in Plymouth, there had been a flood disaster on the east coast of England. The Royal Marines on board were requested to help at the disaster at Canvey Island. Shortly after they had agreed to do so, they were told they could not

23

take these remaining assault and landing craft, because they were radioactive. However, these same craft, which were secured on the upper deck and some in the tank space, were used as sleeping accommodation by many men. I myself slept in a wooden box in the tank space among the radioactive craft. The laboratory had been dismantled and winched back to the bulkheads for the return voyage.'

Back in England, Mabbutt and the rest of the crew were set to work stripping paint off the bottom of the ship, chipping it off bit by bit. They were bare to the waist while doing this, even though, according to Mabbutt, 'it was common knowledge that the whole of the hull of the ship was radioactive. The condenser for making fresh water from salt was radioactive, as were the bilges.' After the *Zeebrugge* had been refitted, it was used as an accommodation ship for dockyard workers. Six months after he returned to England, Mabbutt began to suffer from psoriasis – a skin disease – on the forearms. He saw a consultant, who told him it was caused by nerves. Mabbutt was unconvinced. 'I was then a boys' instructor, with absolutely no stress at all.' The consultant did not ask if Mabbutt had attended the Monte Bello test.

Morrie Westwood was also at the first British atom bomb test. He was an able seaman in the Australian navy, serving on board HMAS *Koala*. He watched the test from his ship, at a distance of thirty-nine miles. Soon after the explosion, however, the *Koala* sailed right into the immediate blast area to salvage a barge which had sunk just before the test. Sandy Brennan, a naval diver, went down to the sea-bed to attach lines to the barge, which was then hauled on to the forecastle of the *Koala*.

With the salvaged barge on deck, *Koala* tied up next to a British vessel which had a laboratory constructed on board. The diver, Brennan, went on board the British ship; while walking past the laboratory section, he started the Geiger counters ticking. He was found to be contaminated by radiation from the barge. Morrie Westwood and the rest of ship's company were then tested. They, too, turned out to be contaminated.

'We were told to bathe – I had about six showers – until the scientists were satisfied that we were clean enough to return to the ship, leaving all our gear behind,' Westwood recalled. 'In my case, this was one pair of shorts and one pair of sandals, which were set in cement and dumped at sea. The barge was then hosed down and allowed to remain on deck for the duration of the journey. Dr Penney [chief scientist at the tests] came on board *Koala* and apologized to us for the incident. After a week or so, we headed for Fremantle, where the barge was offloaded and sent back to the UK. We were told not to mention the incident, but on arrival at Fremantle the wharf labourers declared the ship black.'

In 1957, while still in the navy, Westwood was admitted to a naval hospital with a stomach illness, the cause of which, he says, he was never told. After leaving the navy in 1958, he developed psoriasis. The condition was eased by various ointments, but it has never healed.

Clifford Henderson was posted to the Maralinga test site in 1957 as a cook; he was a corporal in the RAF catering branch. When he arrived at Maralinga, a Captain Brown of the Australian Army Catering Corps offered to take him on a tour of the sites where bombs had been detonated. They drove through a manned checkpoint to a bomb crater. As they stood on the edge and looked down into it, Captain Brown told Henderson: 'We'll go no further – it's still hot.' Then he added: 'We've got to keep an eye open. Those abos [*sic*] like camping in these craters.'

Shortly after that, Henderson saw a family of aborigines at the police post at Maralinga. There were three of them – a man, woman and child – and they were wearing garments like loin-cloths. They were carrying spears and billy-cans. 'They were in the company of a number of security personnel, who seemed quite busy with them,' Henderson told the Royal Commission.

Gordon Wilson, who is now a school caretaker in Hull, found aborigines in the 'yellow area' – the most dangerous of the three restricted zones at Maralinga – on several occasions. Wilson arrived at Maralinga in 1957, a year after he had joined the Royal Engineers as a regular soldier. 'There were no briefings at

25

all on what we were doing and what was going on, although people in the camp told us what the nature of the work was,' he recalled. 'After we had been there about a week, we were taken nearer to the forward area and stayed in a tent encampment at Roadside [the name given to one of the temporary camps]. Although we were relatively near the forward area, there were no definite instructions or warnings about any hazards, or about the effects of radioactivity in general. I believe we were about five miles from ground zero.'

Wilson stayed at the Roadside camp for all three blasts he witnessed. 'At some stage,' he recalled, 'we went into what we called the yellow areas to repair and erect some signs on the track. Some of them were danger signs, some were just location signs. We also had to make a large number of things in our workshops, the exact function of which we were unaware of. The only special equipment we had was a radiation film badge, which was replaced at intervals. The winds would change around and a fair amount of dust was blown about in the yellow area. After we had been in the yellow area, we had to take showers. We worked quite near the craters, in that we could see them, but never went right up to one.'

There was little restriction on the men's movement. Every Sunday or rest day, bored with the lack of entertainment or recreation at the camp, Wilson and a couple of friends used to take a Land Rover out of the official pool and go for a spin. They often went dingo shooting, using a rifle which an Australian soldier had given them.

On one occasion, Wilson and his friends came across three aborigines about three miles away from the Roadside camp. 'One of them could speak in a way that was more or less comprehensible to us,' Wilson recalled. 'He told us they were moving around the area. He talked to us about the blinding lights of the explosions, by which we assumed he meant the flash. It was very difficult to understand all he was saying. On this occasion, I gave one of the three a shirt which I had in the back of the Land Rover. We saw them a number of times after that. They would come looking for the Land Rover and we would sometimes give them presents. The one who could speak English best showed us how to set dingo traps.' When Gordon Wilson told his story to the Australian Royal Commission in 1985, he was asked why he hadn't reported it at the time: the aborigines were, after all, in a prohibited area. 'Let's face it,' he replied, 'it was their country.'

Wilson himself was only once turned back on his outings into the prohibited area; an English security man told Wilson that he had come too far and that he must turn back. The rest of the time, however, he roamed the range unhindered. 'We used to climb the observation towers by ourselves. There were a lot of tracks going off away from the main track, which ended up in the bush, and we used to go down these. On the occasion on which we were stopped, we had gone too far towards the forward area. We broke through the bush and saw that everything was levelled off. It was very quiet and eerie, and there was no vegetation. I feel sure that if we had wanted to we could have found our way to the craters, which were in a straight line from the observation towers.'

The Monte Bello Islands, scene of the detonation of Britain's very first atom bomb in 1952, were the setting for two more atomic tests in 1956. Nearly thirty years later, in 1984, the British government admitted that the second of these tests had been a 60-kiloton blast, *three times* bigger than previously stated. Secret documents released to the Public Records Office in 1985 suggested it was even bigger than the 1984 description – 98 kilotons.

Bernard Perkins, who now lives in Dagenham, joined the Royal Navy in 1950. He trained as a radio operator, had a commission in the Hong Kong shore station and then went to Whitehall as a teleprinter operator before joining HMS *Narvik* and setting sail for the Monte Bello Islands.

'I did not know exactly what was happening,' he recalled, 'except that we were going to the atomic tests at Monte Bello Islands. We were told that we would be paid one shilling per day danger money, but we thought that was for the danger associated with the explosion rather than the radioactivity.'

The *Narvik* called at Perth before heading for Monte Bello. It was only after they had left Perth that the men were told that

27

there were atom bombs on board, although, according to Perkins, 'it was in fact obvious by that stage'. The bomb section was on a bulkhead directly beneath the bridge, and it had an entrance fitted with warning lights and bells. The rest of the equipment for the test was in the hold or on deck.

When the ship reached the islands, it moored near the lagoon where HMS *Plym* had been exploded four years earlier. The men were told not to go anywhere near the shore or the site where the *Plym* had been blown up, but one of the *Narvik*'s boats ran aground near the site. In addition, a detachment of Royal Marines had to go ashore to unload the equipment needed for the next test.

Perkins was on duty in the wireless office when the first explosion of this new series took place. He was in touch with two RAF Canberras which were to fly through the atomic cloud, while another telegraphist in a separate room was in radio contact with the scientists on the island and the ship's bridge. At first, according to Perkins, the conversation between the two Canberra pilots was largely technical. 'Then they reported that they were going into the cloud. I distinctly heard one pilot say to the other, "How does the second hottest pilot in the RAF feel?" I thought at the time that this referred to the heat of the fireball rather than radiation.' Perkins kept in touch with the pilots while they flew through the cloud; when they headed for home, he went up on deck and saw the plume of smoke from the explosion.

After the first bomb had been exploded, Perkins and his colleagues were allowed ashore on the islands. 'There was a beer tent where we were allowed to go with our beer to drink it,' he recalled. 'There was nothing to look at and it was boring.' Perkins and a couple of other radio operators asked an army man if they could go to examine the spot where the bomb had gone off. 'He said we could if we wanted and that no one was stopping us. I would estimate this was approximately seven days after the blast.'

Perkins and his two friends set off on foot. 'There had been a slight hill with a tower on it, and the hill had been flattened by the explosion, and the tower had disappeared. There was a fused, glass-like substance on the floor, looking like ice.' The men's dress for this outing could hardly have been less suitable. They were bare to the waist, wearing shorts and sandals. As a gesture to safety precautions, they put their radiation film badges on their shorts.

The run-up to the second explosion of the series was fraught with difficulties. Because of poor weather, there were three or four abortive countdowns. 'Everybody was getting very fed up and one or two sailors were taken off the ship to hospital since they had had breakdowns,' Perkins recalled. 'There was very great tension in the air. I remember talking to one scientist who was working on a timing device. He said that the long wait was because the weather had to be right, but that they had to hurry up because of time and money. He said that the weather was about to close up and the winds change. He said that if the second explosion was going to take place, it would have to happen soon, and that if it did not it would be the most tremendous waste of time and money.'

Perkins was off duty when the second explosion took place, so he watched it from the deck of the *Narvik*, about five miles from the blast. 'There was a big Geiger counter on the aft deck which went berserk after the second explosion. There was also one on the superstructure. My recollection is that it was ticking for a few days after the bomb, weaker all the time.'

On board the *Narvik*, there was a rumour that the fireball from this second explosion had finished very close to the bunker where the scientists had been positioned. The rumour gathered strength on the day after the test, when the ship sailed back into the islands to pick up the scientists. 'I stood on the upper deck watching it,' Perkins recalled. 'A motor boat came towards us. There were two men with protective clothing on and five or six scientists, all of whom had blankets wrapped around them, looking as if they were in shock. I looked down on them from about twenty-five yards away. They were brought to the ship's side and came up the gangplank, and had to be helped up. Nobody saw them again. I believe they were taken from the ship at night. To the best of my recollection, they were wearing sandals, khaki shirts, stockings and shorts, with no headgear.'

'What the bloody hell is going on?'

This was not the first indication that something had gone wrong with the second explosion. On the actual day of the test, when Perkins came on duty at 4 p.m., his job was to transmit reports from the journalists who had watched the blast. Suddenly a signal came in direct from Sydney. It was a message from the acting Australian Prime Minister, Sir Arthur Fadden, to the British Prime Minister, Anthony Eden. It was a very short message and, in the light of what has since emerged about the British nuclear tests, one which might reasonably have been sent somewhat sooner. 'What the bloody hell is going on?' Fadden demanded. 'The cloud is drifting over the mainland.'

CHAPTER TWO

'He ought to stick to science'

Ernest Bevin on Professor Patrick Blackett's advice
not to build the atom bomb

The Australian Prime Minister's frantic signal to London as the atomic cloud drifted over the mainland in June 1956 stands out as one of the few occasions on which the Australian government took issue with Britain over the atom bomb tests. For the most part, Australia was only too ready to offer facilities for weapons testing – one of the few conditions imposed on the British by the Australians during the tests at Emu Field in 1953 was a requirement that, on religious grounds, bombs should not be exploded on a Sunday. The relationship between the two countries in those early days seems to have resembled a marriage between a reluctant bridegroom and a very willing bride: Australia granted Britain's request, in 1950, to be allowed to test her first bomb on Australian territory, and then waited patiently on the sidelines while the British government tried to set up a better deal elsewhere.

The request came in the form of a highly classified message from the British Prime Minister, Clem Attlee, to Menzies on 16 September 1950. It was simple, and in two parts. Would Australia allow Britain's bomb to be tested on her territory and, if so, could the British carry out a survey of the Monte Bello Islands, a site which had been recommended by the British Admiralty?

The background to this request, Attlee explained, was that Britain had already sought permission from the US government to use Eniwetok, an atoll in the South Pacific on which several American bombs had been tested, but was still waiting for a reply. In the circumstances, Britain had no choice but to look around for alternative facilities.

Only three days later, Menzies replied, agreeing in principle to both the atom bomb test and the survey. (Neither the Australian nor the British electorates were to know anything about these negotiations until eighteen months later, when plans were well advanced.) In November, the British survey party set out for the Monte Bellos but the fate of the islands was not yet sealed. The British also investigated seven possible sites in Canada and one, near Churchill, Manitoba, looked promising. It was ruled out because the sea was too shallow to use ships near the shore, and the British had already decided their first test should simulate an atom bomb attack on a harbour.

The survey party which visited the Monte Bellos reported back in January 1951. The four main islands in the group were 'inhospitable', they said, with no shade and no water supply. Dr William Penney, the scientist in charge of the trial, was in favour of using the site, as long as the British navy could cope with the heavy calls which would be made on it – including the provision of an aircraft-carrier fitted with workshops and laboratories, and several other ships.

But even at this point, when the British government asked the Australians for formal approval of a test in the Monte Bellos in October 1952, it had not given up hope of doing a deal with the Americans. The Australian government obligingly gave its formal permission in May, but the British postponed a final decision while they waited for a reply to a further request to use American facilities. In September, the Americans finally made an offer of a joint test programme at their own site in Nevada. Penney flew to Washington to discuss the offer, which he described at the Australian Royal Commission hearings in 1985 into the bomb tests as 'highly restrictive'. In spite of the problems, Penney wanted to accept. 'I would have taken it [the American offer] because I wanted to get back to Anglo-American collaboration,' he said. 'But the British government said no.'

The offer was far from generous. The terms were that the Americans would take delivery of the British bomb, with full details of what was in it, and carry out the test themselves. But Penney, who worked in the US during the Second World War on the Manhattan Project – the massive programme to build the first-ever atom bomb – thought the plan would be cheaper than going it alone in the Monte Bello Islands.

But in October 1951, a general election returned Winston Churchill to power. In December, the British government overruled Penney and made a final decision to choose Australia.

Nearly two months later, on 19 February 1952, the British and Australian governments decided to let their electorates know what they were up to. After much discussion, they issued a joint statement. It succeeded in being at once reassuring and uninformative:

'In the course of this year, the United Kingdom Government intends to test an atomic weapon produced in the United Kingdom. In close cooperation with the Government of the Commonwealth of Australia, the test will take place at a site in Australia. It will be conducted in conditions which will ensure that there will be no danger to the health of the people or animals in the Commonwealth.'

The statement glossed over the fact that no one knew whether the islands were Australia's to offer – they were of little interest until now. And although the islands were uninhabited, they were a rich source of plants, animals and insects – a scientist involved in the bomb tests found over 400 species of plants and animals on the islands, including twenty species of insect never seen before. But the announcement of the project seems to have been well received. In 1952, a public-opinion poll showed 60 per cent of people questioned in Britain were in favour of the bomb, with only 22 per cent against. But the siting of the tests in Australia had no more enthusiastic supporter than the Australian Prime Minister, Robert Menzies.

The one thing Menzies seems to have feared is that Britain would change her mind and go elsewhere. In 1954, a rumour went round that Britain was again thinking of conducting some of her atom bomb tests in Canada. Menzies was beside himself, and had to be placated by the British High Commission in Canberra. A cable to London outlined the High Commission's efforts at smoothing over troubled waters: 'I felt it best to use discretion . . . and scotch any suggestion that we had been thinking of Canada as an alternative,' it said.

So Menzies got his way, and the Australian people played hosts to nine more atomic explosions over the next eighteen months, to add to the three they had already experienced. The Canadians, it now seems, have a lot to thank Robert Menzies for.

The atom bomb which Britain tested in 1952 was her first, in the sense that it was designed and made in Britain. But the bomb which had been built in the US during the war was an international project, with a substantial British input. The Manhattan Project was bankrolled by the US government and headed by an American scientist, Robert Oppenheimer, but many of the scientists who worked on it came from war-torn Europe – Britain supplied nineteen of them to the project's headquarters, the top-secret laboratory at Los Alamos, in New Mexico. They included William Penney, who was to become known in the post-war period as the father of the British atom bomb, and Niels Bohr, the world's greatest living physicist, who fled to England from Denmark in the autumn of 1943. One American scientist estimated that the contribution of the British scientists to the Manhattan Project had shortened the time needed to develop the bomb by at least a year. It was the knowledge gained at Los Alamos which laid the foundation for the development of Britain's own atom bomb after the war, when the US withdrew from collaboration.

To understand why Britain was barred from collaboration in the post-war period, we have to look at the events which led to the making of the very first atom bomb – the device which was tested at Alamogordo, in New Mexico, on 16 July 1945. Britain and the US worked on the bomb during the Second World War because they feared that Hitler's Germany might make one first. Ironically, given the way the bomb was later kept secret, the history of its making powerfully illustrates the extent to which the scientific community depends on the free exchange of ideas. Had scientists from many countries not shared the results of their experiments, the project would have taken much longer than it did.

But the story begins at the end of the nineteenth century. In

1895, Wilhelm Roentgen discovered X-rays in his laboratory in Bavaria. The rays were capable of penetrating opaque objects – a book of a thousand pages, for instance, or human flesh. Roentgen gave this form of radiation the name 'X-rays' because he did not know their cause. Months later, in February 1896, Henri Becquerel found that uranium salts emitted radiation which would blacken a photographic plate. Becquerel's discovery of radioactivity in uranium was followed in 1898 by the identification, by Marie and Pierre Curie, of other elements which emitted radiation in this way, including radium.

These discoveries were not unaccompanied by warning signs. Pierre Curie discovered that a patch of his skin had become very red after he had carried a small phial of radium salt in his pocket for a few days – a clear sign that radiation could affect human tissue. In 1902, a factory worker employed on making and demonstrating X-ray tubes in Hamburg developed a tumour on his hand. A monument in that city to the so-called 'radiation martyrs' records 169 deaths attributable to radiation among radiologists. Marie Curie herself died in 1934 of a blood complaint contracted through exposure to radiation; the same fate later befell her daughter, who carried on her mother's research.

In 1927, five employees of the Radium Luminous Material Company in New Jersey sued for damages after suffering rotting jaws and spines. The women were employed to paint the luminous dials of wrist watches, using radium paint. They used to lick their brushes to a fine point after dipping them into the paint; by 1924, nine of them were dead and many crippled. When the case came to court, Marie Curie was among the well-wishers who sent them messages of sympathy. They settled for lump sums of $10,000, and small pensions.

But the evidence of the horrifying effects of radiation on human beings did nothing to deter the quest for further knowledge. What the rays were composed of, and their relationship to the atom, exercised the minds of scientists throughout Europe, and beyond. The reason for this fascination was that the particles emitted by radioactive substances seemed to offer the first real hope of achieving the impossible – splitting the nucleus of the atom, and thereby liberating vast quantities of energy.

The word 'atom' has a Greek root and means 'indivisible'. Until the end of the nineteenth century, this is exactly what the atom was thought to be – an indestructible piece of matter resembling a golf ball. But the work of physicists was to change this picture irrevocably in the early years of the twentieth century. It was an unprecedented time for physics, with momentous discoveries coming thick and fast as scientists took up each other's exciting new ideas and developed them further. The devastating link between discoveries about the atom and the bomb was to be provided by Albert Einstein.

One of the key scientists in the field was Ernest Rutherford, who was born in New Zealand in 1871 but did his pioneering work in England in the first decades of the twentieth century. Rutherford examined the radiation given off by uranium, and gave the names alpha and beta rays to the two kinds he found. Meanwhile a French contemporary, Villard, discovered a third type, gamma rays.

The significance of this work on the nature of radiation is that it produced the revolutionary new idea that atoms are not indestructible. Radioactivity, it turned out, was the spontaneous disintegration of the nucleus of the atom, throwing out part of itself in the process. Rutherford and Niels Bohr, the Danish physicist who would later work on the Manhattan Project, produced a new theoretical model of the atom which was based on the solar system. In this model, the nucleus takes the place of the sun, and the electrons occupy the place of the planets.

The phenomenon of radioactivity raised the hypothesis that it might be possible to split the atom artificially, with the loss of a small amount of mass from the nucleus in the process. The implications of this possibility only became clear with the publication of a series of papers in 1905 by Albert Einstein.

Einstein said that mass and energy are equivalent – different sides of the same coin – and came up with a formula to measure the amount of energy which would be released by converting one into the other. Einstein's formula, $E = mc^2$, demonstrates how much energy would be released by the conversion of even a small mass. E stands for energy, m for mass, and c for the speed of light. Since c is 186,000 miles per second, it is evident that even if m is small, you will end up with a very large quantity of energy.

Physicists began to cast around for ways of splitting the nucleus of the atom artificially. They tried alpha particles, but found they were usually repelled by the nucleus. In 1932, in England, James Chadwick discovered the neutron, thereby completing the model for the structure of the atom – it was now clear that it consisted of a nucleus made of protons and neutrons, and a number of electrons in its outer structure – and at the same time putting science firmly on the road to what would be known as nuclear fission.

While scientists began bombarding a variety of elements with neutrons, in the hope of splitting the nucleus of the atom in two, many people remained sceptical. In 1933, Rutherford, who had by then been made a peer, told the annual meeting of the British Association that anyone who predicted the release of atomic energy on a large scale was 'talking moonshine'. But in 1935, Frédéric Joliot-Curie, son-in-law of Marie Curie, said that scientists who were able to construct and demolish elements 'may also be capable of causing nuclear transformations of an explosive character... If the propagation of such transformations in matter can be brought about, in all probability vast quantities of useful energy will be released.'

In the end, scientists achieved the splitting of the atomic nucleus without realizing what they had done. In 1934, the Italian Enrico Fermi produced infinitesimal amounts of what he thought were completely new substances by bombarding uranium, the heaviest naturally occurring element, with neutrons. He believed he had produced new, *heavier* elements. It was not Fermi but the German chemist Ida Noddack, who suggested a different interpretation – that Fermi might have achieved a 'new type of nuclear disintegration brought about by neutrons.' At the time, no one took the idea seriously.

Otto Hahn, a German chemist, working with Fritz Strassman, repeated the experiment and found barium among its products. Far from being a completely new, *heavier* element than uranium, barium is actually much *lighter*. Instead of turning into a heavier substance by absorbing a neutron, the uranium appeared to have become much lighter. At Christmas, 1938, Hahn wrote to a former colleague, Lise Meitner, an Austrian physicist who had taken refuge in Sweden from the Nazi persecution of the Jews.

Meitner told her nephew, Otto Frisch, with whom she was spending Christmas, about the results outlined in Hahn's letter. Slowly, they realized the implication of Hahn's finding. They remembered Neils Bohr's description of the nucleus of the atom as similar to a drop of liquid. 'It looked as if the absorption of the neutron had disturbed the delicate balance between the forces of attraction and the forces of repulsion inside the nucleus,' Frisch said later. 'It was as if the nucleus had first become elongated and then developed a waist before dividing into two more or less equal parts in just the same way that a living cell divides.'

The most significant thing about fission, as Frisch decided to call the process, was that the combined weight of its products would be less than that of the original nucleus of uranium. The loss of mass would be only a fifth of a proton – but Einstein's equation had shown that this would be sufficient to produce a great deal of energy.

If Frisch and Meitner were right, it should be possible to detect the energy given off, in the form of a measurable electric pulse. They worked out that the amount of energy released, according to Einstein's equation, should be 200,000,000 electron volts. Frisch devised equipment capable of making an accurate measurement and repeated the experiment. It produced exactly the result they had predicted.

The news that the nucleus of the atom had been split galvanized other scientists. Niels Bohr read the paper written by Hahn and Strassman, explaining their findings, while he was attending a meeting of the American Physical Society in Washington. He told other scientists about it on 26 January 1939, adding details of Meitner and Frisch's theory about fission. Some physicists rushed from the room to repeat the experiment for themselves. Meitner and Frisch published their conclusions in a letter in *Nature*, the British scientific journal, on 11 February 1939.

In 1939, as the countries of Europe moved inexorably towards the outbreak of the Second World War, the release of vast quantities of nucleur energy began, for the first time, to seem more than a fantasy. Meanwhile, as early as 1934, Leo Szilard, a Hungarian physicist, had come up with one of the key ideas for producing sufficient energy to make an atom bomb, that of the chain reaction – when the neutron hits the nucleus of the first atom and splits it, more neutrons are thrown out at the point of fission, which then split further atoms, and this process is then repeated.

In the late 1930s, Szilard became obsessed with the idea that Nazi Germany might be able to solve the problems still standing in the way of the bomb. In 1939, as the achievement of Hahn and Strassman became known and the political situation worsened, Szilard's obsessive quest to persuade the British and American governments to make the bomb took on greater urgency.

He hit on the idea of involving Albert Einstein, then living in the US. He persuaded Einstein to send President Roosevelt a letter, dated 2 August 1939, which predicted that uranium would soon be turned into 'a new and important source of energy'. It said that an atom bomb, exploded in a port, might well destroy all of it, along with some of the surrounding territory. The letter, whether written by Einstein or just signed by him at Szilard's prompting, urged Roosevelt to consider making the atom bomb. It succeeded in persuading Roosevelt to take action – he set up a Uranium Committee which, although it moved cautiously, started looking at the possibility.

What was probably the most vital piece of work at this stage was actually done in England. When war broke out, the German scientist Rudolf Peierls happened to be out of Germany on a visit and he refused to go back. He moved to Birmingham University, where he worked with Otto Frisch, by now also a refugee from the Nazis. In March 1940, the two scientists produced a three-page memorandum for the British government. Margaret Gowing, official historian of atomic energy in Britain, describes it as 'a remarkable example of scientific breadth and insight'. It was, she says, 'the first memorandum in any country which foretold with scientific conviction the practical possibility of making a bomb and the horrors it would bring.'

September 1939 put a stop to the free exchange of ideas between scientists which had made the atom bomb a possibility. Frisch and Peierls were doing their work at the very time when the veil of secrecy was falling on science. Although, to the horror of people like Szilard, papers on nuclear fission were published in 1939, the outbreak of the war brought with it a reversal of the tradition of openness between scientists.

That such a change was inevitable in the circumstances did not prevent it bringing with it far-reaching and baleful effects. The US government developed a proprietorial attitude to anything associated with nuclear energy both during and after the war, an effect which led directly to the arms race which continues today. At the beginning of the war, the US overestimated Germany's capacity to work out how to make the atom bomb; by the end of it, the American government clung obstinately to the illusion that the US was decades ahead of the USSR in nuclear technology and should hang on to that advantage, come what may. Scientists in Britain and the US pleaded with their governments to dispel Russia's suspicions about the West's intentions by sharing nuclear secrets: a course, they thought, which offered the best chance of controlling the terrifying weapons demonstrated at Hiroshima and Nagasaki.

But the US government remained obdurate, and tried to maintain its pre-eminence in the field by closing the doors even to its close ally, Britain. America's illusion of superiority was shattered only four years after the nuclear attack on Japan: the USSR exploded its first bomb in Soviet central Asia in August 1949. But by then the damage had been done and the arms race was already well under way.

Towards the end of the war, it became clear from intelligence reports that Hitler's Germany was a long way from making an atom bomb – its efforts had been hampered both by the exodus of scientists from Germany and by a decision to use a technical process which required a substance called heavy water, the greatest supply of which had been successfully removed from France just before the German invasion. The US government's motives in going on with the Manhattan Project, after the removal of the threat which gave birth to it, are a matter of conjecture. On the one hand, work was stepped up so that the bomb would be ready to drop on the Japanese before the end of the war. At the same time, General Leslie Groves, the army engineer in charge of the project, told scientists in 1944: 'You realize that all our work is against the Russians?' One scientist who had gone to work on the project from a British university, Polish-born Joseph Rotblat, remembers to this day the effect this revelation had on him. 'To me, this came as a terrible shock. The Russians were our allies. Thousands were dying every day stemming the advance of the Germans. I never really got over that.'

Nevertheless, at the outbreak of the war, the scientists who pushed their governments to make the atom bomb did so out of fear and loathing for Hitler. In Birmingham, Otto Frisch and Rudolf Peierls worked on their famous memorandum, which was to offer striking new solutions to a number of the technical problems involved in making the bomb.

British scientists had been trying to work out a way of making a bomb from uranium, the heaviest naturally occurring element. To understand the problems to which Frisch and Peierls now suggested answers, we have to return to our model of an atom as a miniature solar system consisting of a central nucleus of protons and neutrons, with a number of electrons in its outer structure.

Which element an atom belongs to is determined by the number of protons in its nucleus – an atom of carbon, for instance, always has six – and this number is balanced by an equal number of electrons. But an element can occur in different forms, known as isotopes, which behave slightly differently from each other. What differentiates one isotope from another is the number of neutrons in the nucleus, the number of protons remains constant, and they acquire their names by the addition of the protons and the neutrons.

The two isotopes of uranium which were exercising the minds of scientists at the outbreak of the war were Uranium 235 and Uranium 238. U235 atoms split much more readily when bombarded by neutrons but form only 0.7 per cent of naturally occurring uranium, the remainder being U238.

Scientists believed that bombarding natural uranium with

neutrons would split insufficient atoms to start the chain reaction necessary for a nuclear explosion. Even if the problems could be overcome, very large amounts of rare uranium, running into tons, would be needed. The Frisch–Peierls Memorandum suggested that a much smaller amount of uranium – as little as a kilogram – would be needed if the U235 could be separated out from the U238. They also came up with a possible method of carrying out the separation.

The paper ended with a prophetic description of the horrors of the bomb that might be made from this process. They estimated that, one day after the explosion, the radiation would be equal to that from one hundred tons of radium. A cloud of radioactivity would kill everybody 'within a strip estimated to be several miles long'. Rain would make the situation worse by carrying radioactive material firmly down to the ground, where it would linger. 'Effective protection is hardly possible,' they wrote. 'Houses would offer protection only at the margins of the danger zone.' Deep cellars might be comparatively safe, but even this protection would depend on access to uncontaminated air.

As a result of the Frisch–Peierls Memorandum a sub-committee of the Committee for the Scientific Survey of Air Warfare was set up. The sub-committee, whose brief was to look into the possibility of a uranium bomb, was given an uninformative title – The Maud Committee.

The name, deliberately intended to obscure its activities, was based on a misreading of a telegram from Niels Bohr to Otto Frisch. Bohr sent the telegram to England as Germany invaded Denmark; it ended with the curious phrase, 'TELL COCKCROFT AND MAUD RAY KENT'. The reference to John Cockcroft, a scientist working in the Ministry of Supply, was comprehensible, but the last part of the message was a puzzle. Frisch and Cockcroft worked out that it might be a garbled anagram of RADIUM TAKEN, a message that the Germans had snatched Denmark's radium stocks. For this reason, a former governess called Maud Ray, who lived in Kent, never received the reassuring message Bohr had sent her about the safety of his family. The phrase preyed on the scientists' minds, however, and the committee ended up with the name Maud. (Much later, it turned out that the name had been ingeniously interpreted by civil servants as an acronym for Military Application of Uranium Detonation.)

Under the supervision of the Maud Committee, work on the feasibility of the bomb project began in April 1940. Many of the scientists who made important contributions at this time were later to carry on their work in the US as part of the Manhattan Project.

The nerve centres for the work were Oxford, Liverpool, Cambridge and Birmingham. A team based at Oxford worked on the separation of U235 from natural uranium. Frisch joined Chadwick at Liverpool, leaving Peierls behind in Birmingham. Peierls's team was soon joined by the German, Klaus Fuchs, who played an important role in work on the size of the bomb. The importance of all this work cannot be overstressed. Robert Jungk, in his history of the first atomic scientists, *Brighter than a Thousand Suns*, wrote: 'The countless administrative and technical obstacles which blocked the road to the release of atomic energy were finally overcome simply and solely by the determination and obstinacy of the scientists resident in the Anglo-Saxon countries... They repeatedly took the initiative in bringing that mighty weapon into the world.'

Just over a year after the setting up of the Maud Committee, in the summer of 1941, it produced two reports. One was on the use of uranium for power, the other on its use in a bomb. The bomb report showed how far matters had progressed. 'We have now reached the conclusion that it will be possible to make an effective uranium bomb,' it said, going on to estimate that a 25 pound bomb would produce the effect of 1,800 tons of TNT.

Margaret Gowing has written that 'there is no doubt that the work of the Maud Committee had put the British in the lead in the race for a bomb.' If it had not existed, she says, 'the Second World War might well have ended before an atomic bomb was dropped.'

Until the autumn of 1942, there had been considerable cooperation and exchanges of information between Britain and the US about work on the atom bomb. In October 1941,

President Roosevelt had been told of the Maud Committee's conclusion that a uranium bomb was feasible. He decided to speed up the American effort and increase the flow of information to and from Britain. On the day before the Japanese attack on Pearl Harbor, which took place on 7 December 1941, and brought the US into the war, scientists in the uranium section of the Office of Scientific Research and Development were informed of the new programme.

Early in 1942, a British mission visited the US and reported back that the Americans were looking at both the uranium bomb and one based on the recently discovered heavier element, plutonium. Research in the US had clearly raced ahead after its early period in the doldrums. In the autumn of 1942, the American project had reached the point where a major reorganization was needed to cope with its huge industrial requirements. A special group of the US Army Corps of Engineers, known as the Manhattan District, was given charge of the project, under the overall leadership of Leslie Groves. At this point, Britain's problems with her major ally started with a vengeance and provided, if the British had only known it, a foretaste of what was to come immediately after the war. The underlying cause of the trouble was the question as to who would control nuclear energy after the war.

How much the exclusion of Britain from the Manhattan Project between 1942 and 1943, and from the American nuclear energy programme after the war, rankled on this side of the Atlantic can be gauged from Leonard Bertin's history of the period, *Atom Harvest*. 'British scientists who, with full approval of their Government, had been ready to provide the Americans with all the data they wanted, suddenly found doors closed upon them,' he wrote in 1955. 'There is a popular but mistaken belief that this breakdown in cooperation occurred after the war with the passing of the McMahon Act [the act which forbade US scientists to share information] in 1946. It would be truer to say that it started the day the Americans were persuaded that, despite their own misgivings, the production of atomic weapons before the end of the war was possible.'

The British were informed of the new, restrictive conditions for collaboration at the beginning of 1943. Effectively, they were told that they would be expected to continue to supply full information on the parts of the bomb effort on which they were working. The information which the British would be given in return was severely limited. For instance, Britain was to receive no information at all on one of the main methods of separating out U235.

According to Bertin, the excuse given to the protesting British was security. But, he writes, 'subsequent events indicated quite clearly that the question mainly at stake was that of post-war development of atomic power.' The British government certainly seems to have believed this to be the underlying cause of the rift, because the way found out of the impasse conceded to the Americans the final say on post-war developments in nuclear matters with commercial applications.

The Quebec Agreement, signed on 19 August 1943 by Roosevelt and Churchill, agreed that, 'in view of the heavy burden of production falling upon the United States as a result of a wise division of war effort, the British government recognise that any post-war advantages of an industrial or commercial character shall be dealt with as between the United States and Great Britain on terms to be specified by the President of the United States to the Prime Minister of Great Britain.' Churchill disclaimed any interest in these possible commercial aspects 'beyond what may be considered by the President of the United States to be fair and just and in harmony with the economic welfare of the world'.

For this high price, collaboration was restored and, towards the end of 1943, teams of scientists from Britain got ready to go to the US, some to work at the nerve centre of the Manhattan Project, the top-secret laboratory set up at Los Alamos, in New Mexico, under the direction of the American physicist, Robert Oppenheimer. The British thought it was worth it because their own resources were severly stretched by the war effort, and sites in Britain would be vulnerable to enemy bombing. They were probably right: the knowledge gained at Los Alamos and elsewhere would prove invaluable after the war.

The British scientist who knew most about the Los Alamos bomb project was William George Penney. Penney was thirty when the war broke out in 1939. Pictures of him in the 1950s, when he was a national hero, show a large, even shambling figure, straight hair brushed sideways across an unusually square head. The man who gave evidence at the Australian Royal Commission hearings in January 1985 was a smaller but equally solid figure. What seemed little affected by age – he was seventy-five at the time – was his curiously slow manner of speech, familiar from thirty-year-old newsreels when excited reporters hung on his every word.

In 1952, Churchill's telegram of congratulation on the success of the first British atom bomb test at the Monte Bello Islands made Penney a knight with the words, 'Well done, Sir William.' In 1967, he became a life peer, with the title Baron Penney of East Hendred. He now lives in the village of East Hendred, a stone's throw from the atomic research establishment at Harwell.

Penney's statement to the Australian commission deals mainly with the period from 1947 to 1959. His involvement with the Manhattan Project is covered in two laconic sentences: 'During the war, I was recruited to the US Manhattan District Atomic Weapon Project. I made measurements of the yields of some of the early US tests and visited Japan to report on the damage caused by the two weapons used at Hiroshima and Nagasaki.' But Penney's role was a key one as far as the British were concerned.

At the start of the Second World War, Penney was an assistant professor of mathematics at Imperial College in London. He went to school in Sheerness, Kent, and gained both a BSc and a PhD at London University. Other degrees followed, from the University of Wisconsin, from Cambridge, and from London. At Imperial, Penney had been working on the nature of matter and had published numerous papers on the structure of various elements and compounds.

From 1940, he was on loan from the college to the Admiralty and the Ministry of Home Security to do war work; he was asked to look at the effects of an underwater explosion, particularly the effect known as the pressure wave. This work later influenced the setting up of Britain's first atom bomb test, since Penney was anxious to discover the effect of an atom bomb explosion on board ship in a harbour.

Penney went on from this work to examine the effects of explosions in air on ships, houses and other vulnerable structures. Next, he advised the Admiralty on the kind of pressures to which the temporary harbour to be used for the Normandy landings would be exposed. In 1944, he went to Los Alamos.

Penney was asked to go to the US, well after the first wave of scientists from Britain arrived, because the project needed someone expert in calculating the effects of explosions. He worked on areas of the project which gave him extensive knowledge of atom bombs – not just the effects of blast but also the planning of the first bomb test, and the flights over Japan when Hiroshima and Nagasaki were bombed. Chapman Pincher, speculating in a book published in 1948 about whether Britain would make its own bomb, wrote that Penney 'is said to know more about the atom bomb than any other British scientist', making him the most likely candidate to head the project.

When the bomb was dropped on Nagasaki, Penney was in the observer plane with a specially adapted camera to take photographs, in the hope of estimating the size of the bomb, but cloud over the city prevented him. Penney and the other British observer, Group Captain Leonard Cheshire, had wanted to fly in the observer plane over Hiroshima but had been prevented by the local US commander.

So keen were the Americans on Penney that they invited him to attend their first post-war atom bomb tests, an operation called Crossroads, at Bikini Atoll in the Pacific Ocean in 1946. At these tests, in July that year, he was given the title Coordinator of Blast Measurement.

With all this useful experience, Penney was the natural choice to run Britain's post-war bomb project. He was given the task of designing, building and testing the bomb in May 1947, more than two years before the USSR startled the world by testing the first Russian bomb. Leonard Bertin, who interviewed Penney for his book on the early years of the British nuclear programme, published in 1955, was troubled by an incongruity between Penney's personal charm and the work he was doing: 'With his boyish face, blue eyes, tousled, sandy hair and ingenuous smile, he looks the last person in the world to develop a fearful weapon of destruction.'

But it was a job Penney fulfilled single-mindedly and apparently without hesitation. He gave his reason in a brief and rather testy answer to a question at the Australian Royal Commission hearings in London in 1985. 'I thought we were going to have nuclear war,' he said. 'The only hope I saw was [that] there should be a balance between the East and the West. That was why I did this job, not to make money. What I wanted was to be a professor.'

Demonstrating the power of the bomb by testing it unannounced, by devastating two Japanese cities, and by testing it again at Bikini had, of course, more to do with showing off the West's superiority than keeping a non-existent balance. Many scientists realized fully the dangers of this course – Robert Oppenheimer, the scientist in charge of Los Alamos, devoted himself at the end of the war to the problem of how to set up a regulatory agency for the post-war period.

Unlike Penney, some of the British contingent at Los Alamos did have doubts. Joseph Rotblat left the Manhattan Project before the end of 1944 when he knew that Hitler was not going to get the bomb – and because he feared the US intended to exploit its nuclear advantage in a conflict with Russia. He has since campaigned consistently against nuclear weapons. Earlier in 1944, the great scientist Niels Bohr, whose key work with Rutherford had determined the structure of the atom, had come to the view that the only way to prevent a catastrophic war between East and West was a form of international regulation of the atom which would involve some sharing of nuclear secrets with the Russians. In a memorandum to President Roosevelt in July 1944, he urged that 'the terrifying prospect of a future competition between nations about a weapon of such formidable character can only be avoided through a universal agreement in true confidence.'

Bohr wanted the Russians to be told about the existence of the atom bomb before it was dropped. To keep it secret would appear to justify the USSR's suspicions of American intentions, he believed, and would wreck the hope of any post-war co-operation to control it. Bohr succeeded in obtaining personal interviews with both Churchill and Roosevelt. The result was disastrous, and presaged the attacks that would be made on scientists worried by the bomb in the 1950s: the politicians became convinced Bohr himself might be a security risk.

They were certainly not going to give up the massive advantage they believed Britain and the US to have. Churchill wrote to Lord Cherwell, his scientific adviser, that he thought 'Bohr ought to be confined or at any rate made to see that he is very near the edge of mortal crimes.'

Meanwhile, Leo Szilard, who had persuaded Einstein to write to Roosevelt in 1939 and had worked on the Manhattan Project, was equally worried. On 11 June 1945, just over a month before the first bomb was tested at Alamogordo, Szilard and six other scientists from the University of Chicago sent a report to the US Secretary of War: the Franck Report. It took its name from the chairman of the committee set up to produce it, the Nobel Prize-winner James Franck, and warned that an unannounced attack on Japan would deeply shock not only Russia but allied and neutral countries. 'If the United States were to be the first to release this new means of indiscriminate destruction on mankind, she would sacrifice public support throughout the world, precipitate the race for armaments, and prejudice the possibility of reaching an international agreement on the future control of such a weapon,' it said.

In 1946, Albert Einstein joined in the warnings. 'Today we must abandon competition and secure cooperation,' he said. 'This must be the central fact in all our considerations of international affairs; otherwise we face certain disaster.' If he had known the Germans were so far from getting the atom bomb, he said, 'I would never have lifted a finger.' In April 1957, eighteen German scientists issued a statement that none of them would work on 'the production, the testing, or the stockpiling of atomic weapons in any manner'. Two of the signatories were Otto Hahn, whose letter to Lise Meitner in 1938 led to the realization that nuclear fission had been achieved, and Max Born.

Born had, in the early 1930s, been part of a brilliant group of scientists at Göttingen which was broken up by Hitler. Born took refuge in Edinburgh. During the war, his principles did not allow him to take part in war work. But one of his students, also a refugee from Germany, went to work first with Rudolf Peierls in Birmingham, then at the Manhattan Project. He was Klaus Fuchs.

When Fuchs was arrested in 1950, he was head of the theoretical physics section at Harwell. His father, Pastor Emil Fuchs, later posed the question as to whether his son had not been acting more in the interests of the British people than their government when he passed secrets to do with the atom bomb to the Russians. Alan Nunn May, a British scientist who was convicted of spying in 1946, said he gave the Russians information about nuclear power because he did not believe nuclear energy should be confined to the US.

The development of the atom bomb led former colleagues to take such divergent roads that they found themselves in bitter conflict with one other. It is against this background that the subsequent actions of members of the British team at Los Alamos – Bohr, Rotblat, Fuchs and Penney – must be judged.

By the summer of 1945, the Los Alamos laboratory had come up with not one but two types of atom bomb. One, the innocuously-named Little Boy, was what might crudely be called a uranium gun bomb. The other, Fat Man, was a plutonium implosion weapon. The principles on which they were based are simple.

The uranium bomb, Little Boy, used the principle that an explosion would take place as soon as an amount of material greater than critical mass – the quantity required for a self-sustaining chain reaction – was put together. Two lumps of U235 were to be placed at opposite ends of a gun barrel and one would be fired into the other to start the nuclear explosion.

The plutonium bomb, Fat Man, was expected to work by a different method: an amount of plutonium, smaller than the critical mass, was surrounded with high explosives. On detonation of the conventional explosives, the force of the blast would compress the plutonium into a very dense ball in which the chain reaction would start.

Scientists had greater confidence in Little Boy than in Fat Man; they pressed Oppenheimer to allow a full-scale test of the plutonium bomb. After looking at several sites, including various islands off the coast of California, the Alamogordo bombing range in New Mexico was selected. It was already in use to train US Air Force bomber crews before posting overseas.

A cover story was prepared about an unexpected explosion at an ammunition dump in case the intensity of the explosion provoked unwelcome questions from people in the surrounding areas. Fat Man, encased in an outer shell twelve feet long and weighing nearly 10,000 pounds, was hoisted to the top of a 100-foot metal tower. Oppenheimer, who had given the test the name Trinity, watched from the control point five-and-a-half miles away. The test was scheduled for 5.30 on the morning of 16 July, 1945.

Otto Frisch stood with his back to the bomb, about twenty miles to the north. 'I looked at the hills, which were visible in the first faint light of dawn,' he wrote later. 'Suddenly, and without any sound, the hills were bathed in brilliant light, as if somebody had turned the sun on with a switch . . . The hills appeared kind of flat and colourless, like a scenery seen by the light of a photographic flash . . .

'After that [the light starting to diminish] I turned round and tried to look at the light source but found it still too bright to keep my eyes on it. A few short glances gave me the impression of a small, very brilliant core, much smaller in appearance than the sun, surrounded by decreasing and reddening brightness with no definite boundary, but not greater than the sun. After some seconds I could keep my eye on the thing and it now looked like a pretty perfect red ball, about as big as the sun, and connected to the ground by a short grey stem.'

As Frisch watched, the ball rose, remaining connected to the ground by a stem. It flattened out and 'a hump grew out of its top surface and a second mushroom grew out of the top of the first one, slowly penetrating the highest cloud layers.' When he thought the blast wave was about to arrive, he sat on the ground with his fingers in his ears. 'Despite that, the report was quite respectable and was followed by a long rumbling, not quite like thunder but more regular, like huge noisy waggons running around in the hills.' As Robert Oppenheimer watched the successful test, he remembered a line of the Hindu epic, the Bhagavad Gita: 'I am become death, the shatterer of worlds.'

The bomb had contained five kilograms of plutonium 239. The yield of atom bombs is measured by comparing them with the energy released by conventional explosives such as TNT. The Alamogordo bomb was equal to 17,000 tons of TNT, usually written as 17 kilotons.

Less than two months later, the uranium bomb, Little Boy, was dropped over Hiroshima by a US air force plane called the Enola Gay. It was dropped from a height of 570 metres on a city of 256,000 people. The yield of the bomb was 12.5 kilotons: official figures put the casualties at 68,000 dead, while some Japanese scientists claim as many as 140,000.

Three days later, the US air force plane Bock's Car dropped a plutonium bomb, like the one tested at Alamogordo, over Nagasaki at a height of 500 metres. The bomb's yield was 22 kilotons and the official figure for the dead is 38,000. Some estimates put it at 74,000.

Fifty years had elapsed from the discovery of X-rays by Wilhelm Roentgen to the first use of atomic weapons against mankind. At the time the bomb was dropped on Hiroshima, a number of German scientists were interned in Britain. One of them was Otto Hahn, whose work in 1938 showed that nuclear fission had been achieved. His reaction to the attack on Hiroshima was recorded by another scientist in his diary for 7 August 1945: 'Poor Professor Hahn! He told us that when he first learned of the terrible consequences which atomic fission could have, he had been unable to sleep for several nights and contemplated suicide... At 2 a.m. there was a knock on our door and in came von Laue. "We have to do something, I am very worried about Otto Hahn. This news has upset him dreadfully, and I fear the worst." We stayed up for quite a while and only when we had made sure that Hahn had fallen asleep did we go to bed.'

Clement Attlee's Labour government took office on 27 July 1945. Few ministers in the wartime coalition government had known about the bomb project and its transfer to Los Alamos. Not a single Labour politician had been in on the secret. At the end of the war, the scientists from Britain who had worked on the wartime project expected it to be continued; their discussions centred on technical questions about whether the weapons should be based on uranium, like the Hiroshima bomb, or plutonium, the type of device used on Nagasaki. The Chiefs of Staff told the government that, if efforts to set up a system of international control failed, Britain should develop the atom bomb.

As might have been expected, William Penney played a crucial role in bringing the government to the point of taking an official decision to make the atom bomb. In 1946, Penney was Chief Superintendent of Armament Research at the Ministry of Supply. Against a background of pessimistic attempts to secure international arms control, Penney came up with a scheme for an Atomic Weapons Section in his research department.

Penney's scheme was sent to Lord Portal, who was Controller of Production at the Ministry of Supply. Penney said the section would need to do two types of work: the production of fissile material, and the manufacture and assembly of other parts of the bomb whose function would be to trigger the explosion. The second part of the work could be argued to be conventional weapons research, he wrote, although this could not be maintained with a clear conscience.

As a result of Penney's letter to Portal, the Ministry of Supply agreed that Penney should have this responsibility. This decision was taken *before* the government had formally decided to make the bomb. Portal wrote a memo to the Prime Minister, who raised it with an *ad hoc* meeting of ministers called Gen 163. This meeting, held in early January 1947, was attended by only Clem Attlee, Ernest Bevin, Herbert Morrison (Lord President of the Council), A. V. Alexander (Minister of Defence), Lord Addison (Secretary of State for the Dominions) and John Wilmot (Minister of Supply).

One of the curiosities of the whole affair is that the *ad hoc* committee which gave the go-ahead for the bomb project, Gen 163, was not even the same committee which had been meeting to discuss atomic affairs since August 1945. This committee, which met as Gen 75, had been referred to by Attlee as his Atom Bomb Committee and yet three ministers from Gen 75 did not even attend the Gen 163 meeting.

Gen 163 decided Britain should go ahead with a bomb programme. Penney was told some four months later, in May, and given control of the work, which was to take place under the innocuous title of High Explosives Research. (It was a euphemism which persisted for some years. The Australian Royal Commission was given in 1985 a formerly confidential report which dealt with the meteorological conditions in which the first bomb in the Totem test series in South Australia could be fired: its title was High Explosives Research Report No A32, and its date May 1953.)

If the Attlee government's decision involved moral principles, it does not seem to have given the ministers who took it much pause for thought. Ernest Bevin, for one, did not want to hear any arguments against Britain's acquiring the bomb. When the distinguished scientist, Patrick Blackett, who sat on the government's own Advisory Committee on Atomic Energy, suggested Britain should refrain from developing her own deterrent, Bevin gave the idea short shrift. 'He ought to stick to science' was the reply he scribbled to Blackett's suggestion. Clearly, this was not the sort of advice the Advisory Committee was supposed to be giving.

On 12 May 1948, an MP called George Jeger asked a question of the Minister of Defence, A. V. Alexander, in the House of Commons. The question was a plant: its object was to allow the Labour government to admit it was making atom bombs with as little fuss as possible. Was the minister satisfied, Jeger asked, that 'adequate progress' was being made in 'the development of the most modern types of weapon'?

'Yes, sir,' Alexander replied. 'As was made clear in the Statement relating to Defence 1948, research and development continue to receive the highest priority in the defence field, and all types of weapons, *including atomic weapons*, are being developed.' (My italics.)

The spirit in which the Labour government made this admission can be judged by the event which accompanied it. This was the gagging of the press by the issuing of a D-notice which forbade reference to the type of atomic weapons being developed, where the work was being done, who was doing it, and where the weapons were to be stored.

Margaret Gowing has said that the Prime Minister, Clem Attlee, and the Foreign Secretary, Ernest Bevin, became 'paranoic' about the release of information on the atom bomb programme. It was also the case, she said in a film on the nuclear industry, *Unstable Elements*, that 'the press really probed very little and the public suffered as a result'.

How far journalists would have got, if they had had the inclination to do a bit of investigating, is doubtful. The decision that Britain would build the atom bomb was taken in conditions of such secrecy that many members of Attlee's cabinet were not privy to it. Even after the public announcement, if A. V. Alexander's throwaway line deserves to be counted as such, ministers managed to conceal from parliament what they were spending on the project: when Churchill returned to power as Prime Minister in October 1951, he was astonished to discover that the Labour government had covertly spent nearly £100 million in this way, unbeknown to the House of Commons.

After a brief pause, Churchill decided to honour this useful tradition. On 4 March 1954, a Cabinet committee chaired by Churchill agreed to conceal the extent of the nuclear weapons project by hiding it under innocuous headings like 'other current expenditure' and 'extra-mural research'. Churchill's government also decided that, although its decision in July 1954 to develop the hydrogen bomb would undoubtedly offend many British people, it was Attlee's government which had set Britain on this rocky moral road in the first place: 'insofar as any moral principle was involved, it had already been breached by the decision of the Labour Government to make the atomic bomb,' Cabinet papers record.

At the time Gen 163 was taking its historic decision in January

1947, Britain was discovering how little help would be forthcoming from its wartime ally, the US. At the end of the war, Britain had rested hopes of cooperation on the Hyde Park Agreement, signed by Churchill and Roosevelt in 1944. This said that full collaboration would continue after the defeat of Japan until ended by *joint* agreement.

After Roosevelt's death, the British discovered that no one else in America seemed to know about it. But when Attlee flew to the US in November 1945, the result of talks with President Truman and the Canadian Prime Minister, Mackenzie King, seemed encouraging. An agreement was signed which said, 'There shall be full and effective cooperation in the field of basic scientific research among the three countries.'

In February 1946, Britain put the new agreement to the test by asking the Americans for information about building the piles needed to produce plutonium – the American government at this time knew far more about Britain's atomic plans than the British people or even, for that matter, a sizeable chunk of the British Cabinet. The US wanted Britain to build its piles in Canada; Britain, the Americans said, was too vulnerable to enemy attack. The British government refused and found that the information it needed was not handed over. Three months later, Britain did manage to secure an agreement with the US which assured its access to uranium ore – less than twelve months later, movements of uranium became the subject of a D-notice in Britain.

In August 1946, the possibility of cooperation with the US was abruptly extinguished. An act on the control of atomic energy in the US, named after its sponsor, Senator Brien McMahon, became law in that month. Clause 10(a) introduced restrictions on the sharing of a wide range of data about atomic energy. McMahon later said he had discovered the existence of secret agreements between the US and Britain only after the bill became law. Nevertheless, the effect of the act was, as Leonard Bertin wrote in 1955, to create 'a fantastic situation in which the United States completely slammed the door on her British friends'.

Bertin was writing at a time when British feelings about what seemed churlish and ungrateful behaviour on the part of the

Americans were close to the surface. It was certainly the case that Britain had to get on with its own bomb programme more or less unaided until the mid-1950s, when American admiration for the British project promoted renewed collaboration.

But Margaret Gowing stresses that the British decision to make the atom bomb was not taken as a result of the McMahon Act. 'The decision was', she writes, 'a symbol of independence.' Even if relations with the US had been better, Attlee's view was clear: 'If we had decided not to have it, we would have put ourselves entirely in the hands of the Americans. That would have been a risk a British government should not take ... For a power of our size and with our responsibilities to turn its back on the Bomb did not make sense.'

The effect of the withdrawal of US cooperation did have important effects, however. It meant that Britain had to find out for itself, through trial and error, the answers to questions which the Americans already knew. It also led to the testing of British weapons in Australia.

'The inherent stupidity of an independent test in Australia, when the Americans had such well-developed test sites, had led to long meetings and cables and a final transatlantic dash by Penney,' says Margaret Gowing. 'But though the Americans had finally expressed their willingness to help, they had felt bound to impose so many restrictions and conditions under the McMahon Act that the Chiefs of Staff and all the departments concerned had unanimously concluded that the test should be held after all in Australia.'

CHAPTER THREE

Operation Hurricane

3 October 1952, Monte Bello Islands

The 'inherent stupidity' of testing the first British atom bomb in Australia lay in the huge effort required to prepare such a distant and inhospitable site for the explosion. The Monte Bello Islands could not even provide a supply of water for the number of people involved in the test in one way or another – 1,100 British and Australian personnel as the time for the test drew close.

Once again, the British had a lot to thank the Australian government for; the Australian armed forces obligingly helped out with several vital tasks. In February 1952, for instance, the No. 5 Airfield Squadron of the Australian air force, the RAAF, constructed a freshwater pipeline on the mainland which brought water to a jetty near the mouth of the Fortescue river. Throughout the entire operation, all the water needed in the Monte Bellos was taken from this jetty by an Australian navy water lighter across the fifty miles to the islands.

The Royal Navy supplied five ships for the operation, which was given the code name Hurricane. It was carried out under the overall control of a senior naval officer. Ninety-nine scientists travelled by ship to the islands, the majority of them on HMS *Campania*, where relations between the civilians and the navy became decidedly strained. Other scientists, including Penney, were luckier: they flew to Australia in Hastings aircraft and then made the trip from Onslow, on the mainland, to the test site in the Monte Bellos in the Australian ships, HMAS *Hawkesbury* and *Warreen*.

The first two British ships, HMS *Zeebrugge* and HMS *Narvik*, left Portsmouth for the islands on 19 February 1952, one day after the two governments had made their joint announcement of the test in Australia. The two events were not unconnected, as a report compiled by the naval commander after the explosion shows. 'By the time that Phase I ships were due to leave the United Kingdom, it was apparent that news of the operation could no longer be withheld,' it says. 'On 18th February a simultaneous announcement was made by the Prime Ministers of the United Kingdom and Australia... Although no mention was made of Phase I ships, when they sailed on the following day the press accurately associated them with the expedition.'

To the satisfaction of the British authorities, the press then jumped to the wrong conclusion about the exact location of the test. 'The world press gave great prominence to the public announcements and made a general assumption that the trial would take place at Woomera,' the report goes on. 'This speculation was useful in assisting to keep secret the true location.'

Zeebrugge and *Narvik* were essentially troop ships, whose job was to transport the Royal Engineers to the Monte Bellos to prepare the site. They arrived at the islands more than two months later. HMS *Campania*, the aircraft-carrier which had served as a travelling exhibition during the Festival of Britain a year earlier, was designated command and base ship. On 14 May, Rear-Admiral Arthur Torlesse, the overall commander of Operation Hurricane, hoisted his flag on board *Campania* and a second joint announcement was made to the press. It gave the location of the test, and named Penney and Torlesse as the scientific and military leaders of the operation.

Campania sailed on 10 June, with eighty-five Ministry of Supply scientists on board. With her went the most important ship, HMS *Plym*, in which the bomb was to be exploded. The two ships went the long way round, via the Cape, taking two months to get to the Monte Bellos. Throughout the journey, the *Plym*'s cargo was kept a deadly secret – she was carrying all the bomb's components except for the plutonium core. HMS *Tracker*, which was to act as the health monitoring ship, left Sheerness a few days before and took the quicker route through the Suez Canal. She arrived on the same day as *Campania* and *Plym*, 8 August.

Transporting these numbers of quite diverse people to the other side of the world inevitably produced problems. On the journey down, scientists on *Campania* fell out with naval officers over the subject of dress. The scientists were astonished to find they were expected to wear jackets and ties even in the hottest weather. When the navy decreed that ties must be worn at a film show one Sunday evening, the scientists turned up wearing ties but no shirts.

Film shows assumed tremendous importance in keeping boredom at bay. The naval commander, Rear-Admiral Torlesse, reported afterwards: 'At the Monte Bello Islands the cinema was the greatest recreational interest. No amenities or amusements of a civilised port were available and nightfall put an early end to outdoor recreation. No leave was possible after dark and ships' companies, being physically tired after working in the islands, found the cinema an ideal form of relaxation.'

Torlesse does not, unfortunately, tell us which films were provided or how he arrived at his conclusion: 'The films supplied by the Royal Naval Film Corporation were appreciated by all ranks of the Force and played a large part in maintaining a high morale. The programmes had a high average standard of entertainment value.'

Before they left England, the scientists in charge of the weapon test recognized that conditions on the Monte Bellos would be difficult, even dangerous. One thought that two or three serious accidents among their number would be unsurprising, given the hostile nature of the environment – choppy seas and unwelcoming terrain. But the services and the government took a more robust view. Air Vice-Marshal Davis, at the Ministry of Supply, thought the operation would be 'a grand experience combined with the fun of a picnic'; the government adhered to the opinion that taking part in an atom bomb test was a perfectly normal part of service life.

The insurance arrangements for the test reinforce this view, which depends on an expansive interpretation of the phrase 'normal duties'. The Treasury agreed to honour insurance policies covering the lives of both service and civilian personnel if they were invalidated by their participation in the test. It also insured *civilians* at the test for five times their annual salary. This clause specifically excluded service personnel, however, as 'their normal duties are regarded as covering this employment'.

Insurance cover taken out by the Treasury was valid for only seven years after the test. At the Australian hearings in London in 1985, a British lawyer pointed out that this was of little use, since the latency period – the time which it takes to develop – for radiation-induced diseases like leukaemia and cataracts is much more than seven years in both cases. Penney refused to be drawn on the subject. 'You are asking me to speculate,' he said. 'It is impossible to answer because at the time we did not know what we know now.'

The government claimed at the time of the Hurricane test that 'attributable rates of pension' would apply to servicemen injured in the test; this clause has turned out to be a hollow promise for the majority of ex-servicemen who have since tried to get pensions for illnesses they believe they have suffered as a result of the bomb tests. The Treasury also decided that 'the widow of any officer would not be entitled to the "killed in action" gratuity,' which seems a little mean, given the scientists' view that the operation might well result in people being killed.

The bomb that was tested in a lagoon off Trimouille Island, in the Monte Bellos, was based on Fat Man, the plutonium implosion device which devastated Nagasaki. Its purpose was twofold: to assess the effects of an atom bomb attack on the Port of London, and to establish that Britain could build a bomb unaided.

A month after the successful test, Penney made a radio broadcast. 'When the planning began,' he said, 'a lot of thought was given to deciding which type of explosion would provide information and experience of the greatest value. Purely scientific measurements are most easily made when the weapon is placed at the top of a high tower, but there were other weighty considerations. The Civil Defence authorities in this country badly needed more data about atomic explosions and accordingly the test was planned to get as much novel information as possible for Civil Defence. The decision was made to explode the weapon in a ship moored near land, thus simulating an explosion in a port.'

Penney described himself coyly as 'a scientist who took part in the trial'. He said virtually nothing about the bomb. 'Now for the weapon itself,' he began promisingly, only to go on, 'about which, of course, I can say little. You no doubt realize, if only from the cost of all large atomic energy projects, that the weapon is a complex affair involving specialists in many fields of science and engineering. The fissile material and all the equipment used at Monte Bello were made in Britain.'

The British government did not release figures showing the yields of the bombs detonated in Australia until 1984. Only then did it become clear that the very first bomb was one of the largest in the entire series of tests. At 25 kilotons, the equivalent of 25,000 tons of TNT, it was bigger than either of the bombs used against Japan, and among the British bombs it was the second biggest.

Penney commented in his broadcast that the explosion 'had some resemblance to that of the atomic weapon exploded by the United States in the waters of the Bikini Lagoon'. In fact, the Hurricane explosion was designed to replicate a phenomenon first observed at this US test in 1946. It was called 'base surge'.

The second Bikini test had shown that when a bomb exploded underwater, a huge quantity of water was thrown into the air, where it formed a column contaminated with the products of the explosion. When the column started to fall back to earth, it spread out rapidly and contaminated a wide area. Penney later described it as 'for all the world like a thin pancake mixture spreading as it is poured into a frying pan'.

The Hurricane test, Penney said later, went according to plan. The cloud rose to just over two miles above the sea, the great weight of mud and water preventing its rising further. 'We know what happened and we can give the Civil Defence authorities some accurate answers to some of their problems,' he said.

The team which built the bomb had started off as the High Explosives Research Section of the Armaments Research Department at the Ministry of Supply. As Chief Superintendent, Penney was in charge of all the Department's work – ships, bombs and high explosives, as well as atomic weapons. But in reality, the HER team was quite separate from the rest of the Department at its headquarters at Fort Halstead, in Kent.

Effectively, Penney told the Australian Royal Commission, the completely new Atomic Weapons Research Establishment came into existence some time before he was officially made its first director in 1952.

'AWRE was formed before then but with all the cloak and dagger stuff going on I was rather a strange person,' he said. 'I was Chief Superintendent, Armaments Research, but inside the establishments we had special compounds which were fenced off.' Work started on the AWRE site at Aldermaston, in Berkshire, in April 1950, and it was ready for its first radioactive work by the end of 1951. But getting AWRE fully working in time was a close-run thing. The laboratory for processing plutonium manufactured at Windscale was ready only six months before the Hurricane test.

The overwhelming air of secrecy, combined with the hurried nature of a lot of the work – the date of the test had been imposed on the scientists by politicians, without much thought about whether the deadline was reasonable – meant that Operation Hurricane sometimes had the air of a Keystone cops movie. In the spring of 1952, the people of Gravesend had the British obsession with secrecy to thank for their blissful ignorance of the fact that a full-scale rehearsal of an atom bomb test was taking place on their doorsteps on the River Thames. It went smoothly, except for a communications problem, which was solved by buying radio-telephones designed for use in taxis.

The most vital component of the bomb, its plutonium core, made a surprisingly perilous journey from England to Australia. It was packed inside a container made of cork, with a bag of dye attached to it, and given into the care of an AWRE scientist, who was to look after it for the three-day flight on board a Sunderland flying boat. If the plane crashed in the sea, the theory went, the bag containing the dye would burst and mark the spot, so that the plutonium could be recovered. If it went down over land, the scientist's instructions were simple: jump out, pull the parachute cord, and hang on to the plutonium for dear life. Luckily, the plane arrived without these plans being put to the test.

With hindsight, Australia was extraordinarily generous in its attitude to the conduct of the first three British tests. Operation Hurricane was carried out under British control, with virtually no say being given to the Australians. This arrangement continued for the Operation Totem tests a year later, in 1953. It was a situation which, in the end, disturbed even the hitherto complacent Australians – in 1955, they belatedly set up their own committee which was to be responsible for the health of the Australian people.

Australia's nuclear watchdog, the Australian Ionising Radiation Advisory Council, known as AIRAC, took an optimistic view of the set-up for the early explosions when it reported in 1983 on the British tests and concluded: 'Although Australian services and scientific personnel were present at all three tests, and meteorological services and consultants were provided for the tests, the decision when to fire rested solely with the British authority. However, it may reasonably be presumed that the authority would have taken into account the views of Australian meteorological officers in determining firing times.'

The question of whether conditions were safe enough to fire the weapon – based on predictions of where the wind would carry the radioactive cloud – was a crucial one. The consequences of a bomb being exploded in the most dangerous conditions possible, which happened at the first Totem explosion, will be discussed in a later chapter. For the moment, it is sufficient to note that the Australians did not insist on retaining a power of veto at Hurricane or the next two tests.

Penney's original idea, in February 1952, was that two or three Australians might be invited to watch Operation Hurricane without having access to details of the weapon or its results. By contrast, he invited the chairman of the Canadian Research Policy Committee to attend the test, with full access.

In April that year, the United Kingdom High Commission formally invited Australia to provide two junior scientists to work on the test; one would work with the health monitoring team after the test, the other would examine its effects on concrete structures. The High Commission also passed on a personal request from Penney to use the scientific services of an old colleague, Ernest Titterton. Titterton, who had been sent from Birmingham University to Los Alamos during the war and worked there at the same time as Penney, had emigrated to Australia in the post-war period.

Britain also asked at this time for the use of laboratory space in Australia. This was provided at the University of Melbourne. As the limited extent of the involvement the Australians were being offered became clear, the Australian Defence Committee became rather uneasy: after a correspondence between Britain and Australia which lasted from the end of April to the end of September, Professor Leslie Martin, Professor of Physics at Melbourne University, was officially given an invitation to attend.

Nine days before the test took place at Monte Bello, the *Daily Graphic*'s Sydney correspondent reported that Menzies had confirmed that he did not even know the date on which the test was due to take place. 'I cannot assist the tests – except by keeping quiet,' he said cryptically. No wonder that the *Daily Graphic* went on to report that 'highest government quarters in Canberra' were criticizing Britain for 'excessive secrecy'. An unnamed member of the Australian cabinet is reported to have told the *Daily Graphic* that 'Britain is treating us like colonials' by withholding almost all information. 'Several ministers are openly piqued that Australia should be asked "to do the spade and shovel work at Monte Bello and then be asked to quit the site,"' the report concludes.

These murmurings from unnamed sources did not improve Australia's position. In August 1954, nearly two years after Operation Hurricane, Professor Martin met officials from the British Ministry of Defence to complain that Australia had not yet been given any information about the Monte Bello test or, for that matter, the two tests which had been carried out in 1953 at Emu Field. The Australian armed forces were unhappy about spending money on a project which brought them no advantage, he said. He also pointed out that the siting of the tests in Australia had become a matter of public controversy in the country itself – if the government was to be able to give assurances that it was keeping a close eye on the safety of its people, it had to be in a position to say it was getting the information it wanted about the tests.

The British officials at the meeting were very sympathetic. The difficulty was a technical one, they said reassuringly. Unfortunately, the relevant reports were just being sent to the printer, and happened to be unavailable for the moment. They would be provided soon. Three weeks later, a committee drawn from several Australian government departments met to consider the demands placed on Australian resources by a decision to allow Britain to construct a permanent weapon-testing site in Australia. *Inter alia*, the committee noted that Britain still had not provided information from Operations Hurricane and Totem. Clearly, strong action was called for. The committee decided to recommend that 'a firm request' be sent to Britain seeking the results of the first three tests.

As it happened, the British themselves had less information about Operation Hurricane than they were to have about any other test in the Australian series. The bomb was the very first tested by the British on their own; it was one of the biggest bombs tested in or close to Australia; it was an underwater burst which was known, from the American experience at Bikini in 1946, to produce heavy contamination. In spite of all these factors, only the most desultory atempt was made to check for contamination on the mainland.

In fact, the conduct of the first British test was far from something to be proud of, in spite of the fawning and uncritical press it got at the time. Air crew were not given protective clothing, nor were they monitored to check their exposure to radiation while engaged on the dangerous job of taking samples of the radioactive cloud; estimates of their exposure are really little more than guesses. Radioactive waste was simply dumped in the sea. The permitted levels of exposure to radiation for personnel at the test were much too lax, while no one even gave thought to limits for the exposure of the Australian public. The four main British ships taking part in the exercise became contaminated and were still radioactive when they arrived back in Britain months later; the naval dockyards had no experience at all in how to decontaminate them. The Monte Bello Islands were not properly guarded after the test to prevent chance visitors being exposed to radiation.

Safety measures at the test consisted largely of keeping unauthorized people out of the area and laying down permitted levels of exposure for the people actually involved in the test. The issue of levels of exposure is discussed later in the book; for the time being it is enough to mention two features of the conditions in which Operation Hurricane was carried out. First, no recommendation at all was made about the maximum amount of radiation *members of the public* should be exposed to. Second, the standards adopted permitted personnel involved in the test to be exposed to *six times* the maximum dose laid down for workers in the nuclear industry at home.

The exclusion of unauthorized people from the islands was ensured by a rather cavalier piece of Australian legislation which was enacted in June 1952. The Monte Bellos lie about fifty miles from the north-west coast of Australia. A prohibited zone was declared, extending for a radius of forty miles from one of the islands in the group.

This legislation conveniently ignored the fact that part of the prohibited area was not in Australian waters at all but counted as the high seas. The Australians were subsequently infuriated by an article in the *Daily Mail* in London which queried Australia's legal right to ban foreign vessels from a piece of water it did not control.

Nevertheless, such minor considerations were not allowed to interfere with planning for the test. Sea and air traffic were excluded from the area, and an officer on board HMS *Zeebrugge* was given the power to have people removed from the islands until Rear-Admiral Torlesse arrived and took over. At the same time, a large part of the mainland in Western Australia was declared a restricted area for flying.

A full rehearsal of the test took place on 19 and 20 September; on 1 October, the standby period started. The weapon was detonated by remote control at 9.30 in the morning, Australian time, on 3 October. HMS *Plym*, within whose bowels the weapon had been placed, was vaporized in the blast. Penney watched the test from the flight deck of HMS *Campania*, along with Torlesse and most of the ship's company. They faced away from the explosion as they listened to the last seconds of the countdown being relayed over the ship's loudspeakers.

In a radio broadcast given a few weeks after the test, Penney recalled: 'Suddenly there was an intense flash, visible all around the horizon. We turned to look. The sight before our eyes was terrifying – a great, greyish black cloud being hurled thousands of feet into the air with astonishing rapidity. A great sandstorm suddenly sprang up over the islands. It seemed ages before we heard the bang but, in fact, it was only a minute. Somewhat to our surprise, a second bang – at least as loud as the first – followed a few seconds later. At the same time we felt a peculiar sensation in our ears such as one has in an aircraft losing height rapidly. We were feeling the suction, or reduced pressure, which always follows a blast wave. All the time the cloud was getting higher and higher and assuming fantastic shapes as it was pulled about by the strong winds at different altitudes.

'The explanation of the two bangs heard on the ships and also heard on the mainland is actually quite simple. The first bang was the direct sound wave, and the second was a reflection from a layer of warm air some two miles up.

'Many comments have been made about the shape of the cloud and how different it was from the mushroom cloud with the very high stalk shown in most American pictures of atomic explosions. The great weight of the mud and water in the cloud at Monte Bello kept the cloud from rising very far.'

In fact, the shape of the cloud was a warning of just how unpredictably atomic clouds can behave. Clouds would get lost or they would be blown in unexpected directions, either because the wind changed or because winds were blowing in different directions at various levels. The cloud from Hurricane encountered exactly this phenomenon, as Penney explained in his broadcast: 'The peculiar Z-shape of the cloud ten minutes or so after the explosion was due to the strong winds blowing in quite different directions at different heights. The cloud was pulled into a gigantic spiral shape which, when seen from the ships and from the mainland, appeared rather like a letter "Z", rapidly moving northwards away from the islands and the mainland.'

Penney went on to say that 'the experiment went according to plan'. But the key secret report on Hurricane, compiled by Rear-Admiral Torlesse and released only in 1985, during the Australian Royal Commission hearings, tells a more complicated story. As planned, the early fallout fell into the sea to the north of the islands, and on the northernmost section of the islands themselves. Torlesse records the results of a helicopter survey on the day of the explosion, which showed the area to the north of where *Plym* had been moored to be 'heavily contaminated'. Instruments placed on the northern islands, including Trimouille, confirmed that they must be considered 'dirty' when monitoring teams were being sent out. But Torlesse's report shows that the cloud then behaved so erratically that, by the next morning, most of it was lost; it also shows that part of the cloud broke away and drifted over the mainland not at the expected height of 25,000 feet, but at 10,000, while another piece of it was detected on its way to Fiji.

The operation of tracking the cloud was initially put in jeopardy by what Torlesse calls a 'signal mishap'. As the cloud moved out to sea, he says, 'it was obvious that within a few hours large and increasingly rapid errors in its estimated position were inevitable. In addition, there was an alarmingly large wind sheer in the layers just below 10,000 feet, so that different parts of the cloud travelled in different directions.' Because of these problems, it was decided to start the search for the cloud sooner than planned. A message was sent to Broome, on the mainland, where RAAF planes were waiting to take off. But it took six hours for the secret message to arrive at Broome in 'intelligible form'. It was a stroke of luck that the planes were still able to find part of the cloud, over the sea about 500 miles from the mainland, and collect samples.

A section of the cloud had been expected to travel south-east across the centre of Australia at between 25,000 and 30,000 feet. But on the day of the explosion, weak contamination was detected by an RAAF Lincoln at 10,000 feet near Port Hedland, on the mainland, to the east of the Monte Bellos. The following day, a Dakota aircraft detected a strong signal on radiation-measuring equipment at 10,000 feet in the same area over the mainland. A quantity of radioactive dust was drifting inland over the coast.

No attempt was made to track this section of the cloud further inland or to see if any other parts of the cloud had crossed to the mainland. Only one attempt was made to check for contamination on the ground: two Dakotas flew along the coast at five hundred feet the day after the test but reported no evidence of fallout on the ground. This result is not as impressive as it looks; it was revealed during the London hearings in 1985 that it was realized after the Totem tests in 1953 that an aircraft flying at this height registered only a tenth of the contamination lying on the ground.

None of the aircrew who took part in this sampling and tracking operation wore film badges or protective clothing. The safety measures adopted for the Hurricane test specified that anyone who might be exposed had to have special clothing and be supplied with devices to monitor their exposure to radiation, but an exception to this rule was made for aircrew. Back in 1950, the Air Ministry in Britain had sought the advice of scientists at Harwell on whether there was any risk to aircrew flying through the atomic cloud after the explosion. The answer was that aircrew must avoid flying through the *visible* cloud after the explosion but once the cloud could no longer be seen, there would be no danger.

This advice was later proved to be quite wrong. The cloud sampling operation, which involved the collection of samples in special canisters attached to the plane, was considered at the Totem tests the following year to be an 'unexpected radiation hazard' not only for aircrew but for ground staff dealing with the plane once it had landed. When the sampling canisters were removed from RAAF Lincolns which had flown through the cloud at the first Totem explosion, they were so radioactive that they sent Geiger counters off scale when taken into the laboratory for analysis.

As a result of this incident, Australian aircrew at the later tests were provided with protective clothing and film badges. But at Hurricane and Totem, they had neither; radiation doses received by the crew can only be guessed at by relating them to measurements of the radioactivity in the cloud.

Sampling the cloud was not, of course, the only operation which involved exposure to radiation. Helicopters were used to survey the area close to the explosion; salvage teams were sent on to islands to recover a variety of objects which had been left there to establish the effects of blast; ships sailed into contaminated water for various operations, and radioactive waste was stored on HMS *Tracker* and HMS *Zeebrugge*.

Men involved in 'dirty sorties' – expeditions into contaminated areas – went through health control on board HMS *Tracker* when their duties were finished. Torlesse's report shows that 912 people passed through health control in the twenty-two days after the explosion. Various examples are given in his report of incidents in which men were contaminated.

On the day of the explosion, the only party 'significantly contaminated' was a sortie sent out to recover rocket heads from one of the islands after the explosion. Their hands were judged to be 'dirty'. On two occasions, helicopters were 'mildly contaminated'. The first was on the evening of the day the test took place, when a helicopter flew through a fire on Trimouille Island which had been caused by the blast. In this incident, 'the helicopter crew was also slightly contaminated' and was sent to the health ship for decontamination.

The second occasion happened three weeks after the explosion, when a helicopter was hovering over the sea in the lee of an island and became contaminated by dust blowing off the island. The following day the contamination had to be washed off the aircraft.

Although Torlesse's report is detailed, there is at least one interesting omission from it. He records a number of occasions on which ships sailed into areas where the water was contaminated – HMS *Tracker* detected fallout one mile south of Flag island, directly south of Trimouille, on the day of the explosion, for example. But the fact that the ships were still radioactive on their arrival back in Britain is not mentioned.

The Torlesse report is dated 20 March 1953. Thirteen days before, *The Times* reported an Admiralty announcement that

Campania, Narvik, Tracker and *Zeebrugge* 'still carry some evidence of their association' with the atomic explosion at the Monte Bello Islands. 'Although they were outside the range of the direct effects of the explosion,' the Admiralty said, 'it was necessary afterwards for the ships to enter water which had become contaminated by the radioactive products of the explosion. As was expected, this deposited a certain amount of radioactivity in those parts of the ship coming into contact with sea water, such as the ship's bottom and, inside the ship, saltwater pipe systems and fittings.'

(In fact, a special warning had to be issued to men working in the engine rooms of the ships after intakes were found to have taken in contaminated sea water, the Royal Commission was told by Major-General Alec Walkling in January 1985.)

At the time, the Admiralty went on to say reassuringly that, 'as contact with radioactivity was premeditated and controlled and several months' natural decay has occurred since the event, the residual contamination is now so light as to be almost negligible and does not affect the serviceability or habitability of the ships.'

Even so, to avoid potential risk to the health of men required to carry out repairs in future, the royal dockyards had been asked to remove the contamination. 'Precautions will be taken to obviate health risks to the men doing the work,' the Admiralty stated.

The Times went on to report the cheerful news that 'it was pointed out at the Admiralty yesterday that the effect of the contamination has not prevented the ships remaining in commission since the Monte Bello test, and that all have continued to have complements living on board.'

Torlesse's report does not deal with the implications for the health of the people who lived on the four contaminated ships during the long journey home, or of those servicemen who were still stationed on board at the time of the announcement. If the ships were sufficiently radioactive five months after the explosion to need decontamination, how much more contaminated would they have been in the weeks after the test? Nor does it seem that the Admiralty had a very clear idea of how to deal with the problem, as *The Times* story goes on to make clear.

'The dockyards have had no previous practical experience of this work,' the Admiralty statement admits, but then looks on the bright side. These ships, although only 'lukewarm', 'will provide a most valuable training exercise for the organization which must be set up for the handling and decontamination, should the need arise, of the really "hot" ships which must be anticipated in a future war in which atomic weapons may be used. It will also be an opportunity for practical training for the passive defence organizations.'

It is clear from Torlesse's report that contamination eventually spread from the water around the northern islands in the group southwards for several miles. But this was not the only way in which ships could become contaminated. Torlesse's report reveals that 'a certain amount of gear and equipment used by special parties in the contaminated area, together with some contaminated equipment which was salvaged, could not successfully be decontaminated. Such gear was stored in the radioactive waste store in *Tracker* to await dumping at sea.'

Lightly contaminated protective clothing was kept on board *Tracker* and brought back to Britain for decontamination at home. Rubber boots, and gloves, were cleaned on board ship, where they responded 'fairly well' to treatment to remove radioactivity. 'Heavily contaminated' suits and other woven items were taken off by the people wearing them when they arrived at health control on board *Tracker*.

Heavily contaminated clothing was packed in old cement drums with a sufficient quantity of cement to achieve what Torlesse calls 'negative buoyancy' – in other words, to make them heavy enough to sink. *Tracker* carried twenty tons of cement and twenty tons of aggregate for this purpose. Cementing was done by servicemen on the upper deck under the supervision of health control. The drums were then thrown overboard.

There was also a problem of radioactive waste on board *Zeebrugge*. Effluent from the laboratories, consisting of fresh water which had been used to wash down contaminated items, had to be disposed of. The drums were thrown over the stern of *Zeebrugge*. To the dismay of those on board, the partly-filled drums floated. The solution adopted was simple. The drums were riddled with rifle fire until they began to fill with sea-water and sink.

Torlesse reports: 'The bullet holes permitted the effluent to seep away slowly, after which it would be diluted by the sea, thus ensuring that potentially dangerous concentrations did not remain in the drums for a long period.' Presumably, the same result of contaminating the sea with radioactive waste could have been achieved by simply pouring it overboard in the first place. Perhaps Torlesse had other things on his mind at the time – the return of empty beer bottles, for instance?

The Rear-Admiral gave considerable thought to the question of the type of beer most suitable for operations of this sort. It is a tribute to the British habit of secrecy that his recommendations on this subject appear in a report which bears the classification 'restricted'.

'Canned beer costs one shilling for a 12 oz can and is not as popular as bottled beer,' the Rear-Admiral reports. 'Further, about two per cent of the cans were found to contain flat beer. Australian beer, costing one shilling and threepence (Australian) for a 26 oz bottle, is cheaper and better. The decision to use British beer was taken because of :-
(a) the convenience of canned beer and
(b) doubt about the availability of sufficient quantities of Australian beer.
It is recommended that in any future operation in this area Australian beer should be used. The return of empties is a disadvantage but presents no insoluble problem.'

The concern about the return of empty bottles is touching. Radioactive waste was considered less of a problem, it seems. But the Rear-Admiral was right about the unpopularity of canned beer. Between August and October, 1,100 men in the Monte Bellos drank only 86,400 cans between them – just under one a day each.

Towards the end of Attlee's administration in 1951, the British

Prime Minister told the Australians that the effect of the Monte Bello test would be to contaminate the north-eastern islands in the group, and that contamination might well spread to other islands as well. The area would not be free of contamination for three years after the explosion, he added. During that period, it would be unsafe for human habitation or even visits from the pearl fishermen who had been its only regular visitors before the test.

The question of how to keep people off the islands became pressing as the task force prepared to leave. Penney and a number of his AWRE staff left the islands only six days after the explosion, sailing for Onslow on the mainland in HMAS *Hawkesbury* and then flying to Britain. The process of re-entry to the 'dirty' area to retrieve equipment and take samples was held up for four days from 12 October due to bad weather. Several boats were damaged in gale-force winds – a landing craft sank at its moorings, a motor launch went on the rocks carrying the echo-sounder used for surveying the bomb crater, and a 35-foot pinnace broke loose and was never seen again.

By 23 October, the salvage operation was complete. The Royal Engineers were given the job of dismantling any structures left on the islands to prevent future visitors using them without realizing the danger. Finally, on 31 October, HMS *Campania* led the task force from the Monte Bello Islands to Fremantle.

They left behind the Australian ship, *Hawkesbury*, and an Australian unit whose tasks were to carry out training in radiological safety and to keep people out of the area. The unit set up camp on South East island, less than a mile to the south of Trimouille, with a Land Rover and a wide range of radiation detection equipment supplied by the British. The unit carried out a week of training exercises on Trimouille in early November. They were joined by eleven ratings from *Hawkesbury*, who came ashore for lectures and practical work. The unit left the islands on 16 December: radiation records show they were exposed to about one-fifth of the amount of radiation now permitted for workers in the radiation industry.

After the unit's departure, the security of the islands was left in the hands of the Royal Australian Navy, which made periodic visits and mounted security patrols. In reality, it was impossible for such patrols to prevent the odd landing on the islands, but the security of the area was a pretty low priority for everyone concerned, British and Australians.

Penney was questioned closely on the subject at the Royal Commission hearings in 1985. Whose responsibility was it to keep people out, he was asked? 'I believe it was the Australians',' he replied. 'The advice I gave was that we must be sure that nobody outside . . . no outsiders land on that island for two or three months and that we would review the situation as we went along.'

The account he gave of the decisions that were taken had a haphazard air about it, and lacked any consistency about whether or not there was a risk. At some point, he couldn't remember when exactly, but it might have been three months after the explosion, his chief of staff at AWRE 'came along waving a bit of paper. He said, "The Australians want to take the guard off. Do you think that's all right?" I said, "What's the radiation?"' A bit later, Penney said, he was told that a search party had been to the islands and he heard what levels of radioactivity they had found. They were 'all right', he said, but he insisted that, if the guard was taken away, steps must be taken 'to stop anybody going near the place. So the undertaking was made to put up notices in words in various languages, Japanese being one . . . scary kind of words. Just when that was I can't tell you to the month. It wasn't '52. It could have been middle to late '53. It might have been early '54.'

In the light of these rather loose arrangements, it is not surprising that when a dead body was found on a beach on one of the islands during the Operation Mosaic tests at Monte Bello in 1956, there was a moment's panic until it was realized that the corpse was an old one – that of a fisherman – and had probably been there long before any atom bombs were tested in the area. But even after the Mosaic tests, one of which was the big 98 kiloton blast, the only long-term method adopted for keeping people off the islands was the erection of signs.

This arrangement was accepted in spite of the known fact that some parts of Trimouille Island had posed a radiation hazard *three years* after the first test – and that that hazard was being increased by the addition of contamination from a further two bombs. Nevertheless, the British and Australians decided against any attempt to fence off 'hot' areas in the islands, apparently because to do so would involve all the bother of erecting barbed wire on several islands in the group. Once again, the only hope of chance visitors to the islands avoiding contamination was that they would be able to read, and that they happened to speak one of the languages used on the signs.

When a team from Greenpeace, the environmental pressure group, visited the Monte Bellos more than thirty years after the first test, they found that 'the overwhelming beauty of the islands ... lulled us into a false sense of security about the dangers of visiting a radioactively contaminated area'. At Alpha Island, where one of the Operation Mosaic bombs was tested, 'one would have had to walk on contaminated ground' to read the warning signs. As a general rule, 'the radiation hazard signs around the ground zero [the point on the earth nearest the centre of the explosion] sites were too small in size, difficult to read from a distance and too few in number.'

The Greenpeace team was told, on applying for a permit to visit the islands at Port Hedland, on the mainland, that only six other permits had been issued that year. Yet they encountered four other yachts in the islands in the short period they spent there, suggesting that unauthorized visits regularly take place.

Greenpeace claims it will take sixty years for radiation levels at the ground zeros on the islands to decline to limits recommended as safe for the public. They want contaminated areas to be fenced off and marked with prominent signs warning of the dangers. Since this safeguard was considered 'virtually impossible' in 1956, when the danger was at its height, the chances of its happening now seem slight.

CHAPTER FOUR

'The big bang – for peace'

Headline over *Daily Graphic* editorial, October 1952

'Britain now has what is believed to be the world's most powerful atomic weapon.' This is how the now-defunct *Daily Graphic* greeted – incorrectly – the test at Monte Bello. 'Scientists who saw yesterday's palm-shaped explosion off Western Australia speculated whether it was the first hydrogen bomb that was set off.'

In autumn 1952, Britain was actually nearly five years away from being ready to test the hydrogen bomb. Even the US had not managed it so far; they would explode their first successful hydrogen device, which was far from being a usable weapon, on 1 November 1952 at Eniwetok. The notion that Britain might somehow have been able to leapfrog ahead to the hydrogen bomb is in the realms of science-fiction; British scientists had only just succeeded in meeting the deadline imposed on them by politicians for testing the atom bomb, and the effort had been a massive drain on the country's depleted post-war resources.

The *Daily Graphic* justified its flight of fancy with reference to the opinions of unnamed 'scientists'. It cited the shape of the cloud and the bomb's 'greater and more widespread destructive force on the surface' as evidence. The first is due, as we have seen, to the turbulence of the winds encountered by the cloud. The second is the result of the explosion taking place eight or nine feet under water.

The story's origins can be traced to two motivating forces: the understandable desire of the press to report exciting events even when little hard information is available, and a sense of patriotism which had little outlet in the austere post-war years. With little information flowing from official sources – journalists had to wait three weeks for anything more than bald announcements that the test had taken place – reporters scrabbled around among what contacts they had in the scientific community, puzzled over eye-witness accounts, and cobbled together what they could.

Here is Chapman Pincher in the *Daily Express* of 3 October 1952, reporting 'the facts known in London' about the Monte Bello test: 'The first bomb was almost certainly exploded on the top of a steel tower.' The *Daily Graphic* took the same line, but attributed the information to eye-witnesses on the mainland. 'Reports from Rough Range, North-West Australia, said the weapon appeared to be a bomb exploded from a tower,' it reported rather more cautiously.

The *Empire News*, two days after the test, took an even more imaginative line which clearly stemmed from a hint that the bomb had been in some way intended to supply information for civil defence. 'By the time you read this,' the paper announced, 'British atomic scientists at Monte Bello will have a fair idea of your chances of surviving an atomic attack on Britain.'

Not a bad guess, so far. But now Arthur Morley, writing from Sydney, creates a pot-pourri of facts, guesses and fantasy. The scientists' main reason for coming out to Monte Bello, he goes on, was 'to explode an atom bomb *on top of specially-built new British shelters, mock houses, grounded aircraft, water mains, and electricity cables*. The materials landed for ARP testing, I understand, were *tactical atomic weapons*, atomic shelters, a new British paste or salve to protect the face and hands from flashburn, *injections to minimize the effect on the human system of radiations*, and new simple protective clothing.' (My italics.) These are flights of fancy. It had been a race against time to produce the weapon in time for the Monte Bello trial and there certainly were not spare tactical nuclear weapons lying around to use in tests of this sort. Even more startling is the notion of 'injections in advance of radioactive material in minute doses to attempt to build up immunity', as Morley later describes them. Far from giving immunity, minute doses of radioactive material will themselves cause cancer – there is no way of building up immunity to radiation in the way that there is to some illnesses.

It was not until 23 October that journalists discovered that the

79

bomb had been exploded on board a ship. The Prime Minister's statement to MPs that day triggered off another round of ecstatic newspaper reports. The *Daily Graphic*'s report of the announcement, under the headline 'AMAZING A-BOMB by Churchill', was breathless with excitement.

'Heat 100 times greater than on the sun's surface...' it gasped. 'A 1,450-ton warship vanished in vapour... Thousands of tons of water and rock hurled a mile or more into the air... Then a tidal wave. This is the picture of Britain's amazing first atom bomb explosion as drawn by Mr Churchill yesterday.'

Seven years after the devastation of Hiroshima and Nagasaki, the destructive power of the atom bomb was hardly a revelation. In fact, Britain's Monte Bello test was believed to be the *thirty-fourth* atom bomb exploded in the world. So the gloating tone of the press coverage of the event was more to do with glee at Britain's joining the nuclear club than with the excitement of a new scientific discovery. Newspaper reports were one-sided and uncritical, but they obviously did have uneasy feelings that there might be another way of looking at the development.

The *Daily Graphic* accompanied its enthusiastic news report with a leader uncompromisingly entitled 'The big bang – for peace'. Its clear intention was to scotch the notion that Britain's possession of the bomb was a dangerous proliferation of nuclear weapons which might endanger world peace. 'It is tragic that peaceful nations should be forced to seek continual progress in such terrible agents of destruction,' it intoned solemnly, 'but it is vital that they should maintain a commanding lead.'

A *lead*, note, not the balance of weapons between West and East claimed by Penney. The editorial ended on a note of double dishonesty. 'Both here and across the Atlantic', it said, 'each new atomic achievement brings greater security to the world.' The clear implication was that attempts by Britain and the US to keep in front of Russia in the possession of nuclear weapons were somehow intended to keep the peace, while Russia's striving to catch up was not. It also insinuated that the use of British and American weapons against Russia was unthinkable. But plenty of people did think about it.

In a book published four years before, in 1948, just before
Russia proved to the world that it had developed the bomb,
Chapman Pincher wrote that there was a view, 'widely held by
US citizens and some senators', that 'Britain should help
America to attack Russia now whilst the atom bomb monopoly
remains. There are many people in Britain who believe that the
day of attack is being delayed *only until a sufficiency of atomic
armaments is available.*' (My italics.) So much for the claim that
the West's bomb programme was 'for peace'. (Mercifully, Pincher goes on in his book to say that this enthusiasm for a joint
strike against Russia 'ignores certain political and psychological
features of a democracy which make such an unprovoked attack
virtually impossible'.)

Churchill's revelations to parliament about the Monte Bello
test inevitably reinforced the general air of congratulation that
had already attached to it in the press. Reporters hunted around
for additional scraps of information which would provide further
proof of Britain's status as a nuclear power. In November, the
Daily Graphic ran a story showing that Britain was up ahead in
defending itself from bombs as well as making them. It revealed
that 'after seven years of anxiety, the world now knows there is
something that even an atom bomb cannot harm'.

What can it be? Those 'specially-built new British shelters',
perhaps? Far from it. It's our old friend from Monte Bello, the
British beer can. 'It has at last been revealed that 18,000 cans of
beer suffered the blast from the British atom bomb at Monte
Bello Islands, but came through unscathed', the paper trum-
peted. 'Scientists gingerly approached the potentially lethal stuff
after the bomb went off. They found the tins barely marked.

'They tested the beery contents of the tins for delta rays,
gamma rays, epsilon rays, phi rays – and all the other rays in the
Greek alphabet – and found none.' (This is hardly surprising,
because three of the rays mentioned do not exist.) 'Good British
beer in sound British tins had come through,' the report continues patriotically.

The beer was deemed fit for human consumption – 'so
NAAFI took it back into store and sold it – not gave it away – to
the sailors. They smacked their lips, drank it and said it was less

lethal than much they had come across in their time.' Could this be the reason, one wonders, why Rear-Admiral Torlesse reported that two per cent of the cans contained flat beer?

British beer was not the only toast of the *Daily Graphic*. Penney, as the scientist in charge of the test, became the object of a degree of adulation which is hard to imagine thirty years later. His name became a household word. Newsreels showed him coming down the steps of the plane when he arrived back in Britain. Reporters asked him the kind of questions – 'What does your wife think, Dr Penney?' – now reserved for winners of newspaper bingo games.

The *Daily Graphic* printed an open letter, entitled, 'Thanks, Penney, for the bomb'. 'Dear Dr Penney,' it began, 'Any moment now you will be walking through the door of your modest home at West Norwood, London SE, into the arms of your family, safely back from the successful test of Britain's first atom weapon. (In fact you might be there this morning to read this because your life is so important to Britain that the greatest secrecy is kept about your movements.)

'Britain and the Commonwealth owe a debt – almost impossible to repay – to you, described as "easily the best mind in the world on atom and hydrogen bomb research".'

The next sentence is the key to this fawning piece of journalism. 'The fact that you and your team have made it possible for Britain to make and store atom bombs *has made the country a world-power once again.*' (My italics.)

After all the humiliations of post-war history – scraping to make ends meet, huge loans from the US, learning to live in the shadow of the two superpowers – the bomb had made Britain great again. 'Some people', the *Graphic* conceded, 'doubt whether this is a good thing. Some people, including men eminent in your own form of science, have wondered whether it is the duty of a trained brain like yours to go ahead investigating the mysteries of the universe well knowing that their discoveries could be used for ill as well as good. You had no doubt. You were right.'

The letter then takes up the theme of 'atoms for peace' – the campaign to persuade the world of the beneficial side of nuclear

energy which would be formally launched by President Eisenhower at the United Nations at the end of 1953. American scientists who had worked with Penney, the letter said, 'believe
that a world of wealth, luxury and leisure beyond human
dreams will be possible when atom power is properly harnessed
for our welfare. One told me: "Atom plants must be kept
cool. Great quantities of water are needed. If sea-water is
used then the result is all the priceless salts of the sea are
made radioactive. These could be used to grow food in water,
so that famine need never be seen in the world again."'

The letter continues in this vein, concluding that the atom era
will be 'as though we were stepping out of the Ice Age into a
world of permanent sunshine'. To a world accustomed to reports
of increased rates of cancer near nuclear power stations, and to
the memory of Three-Mile Island, these beliefs seem
dangerously naïve. In 1952, the *Daily Graphic* ended by
expressing Britain's reliance on Penney 'to keep her in the fore-
front of progress and of peace'.

The press had been kept well away from the Monte Bello test.
The nearest anyone got was the top of a hill on the mainland,
ninety miles away. But by the time Britain was ready to test its
first H-bombs, nearly five years later, the government had
become much more sophisticated in its handling of the press. It
even offered facility trips to the trials to journalists, a tactic
which brought with it three major benefits. First, the sense of excitement engendered in reporters who were privileged to act as
witnesses to an exciting event was not conducive to critical or investigative journalism. This was especially important since the
tests were taking place against a background of growing criticism of H-bomb testing. Second, it ensured pages of newspaper
coverage of a scientific development in which Britain was once
again well behind the two superpowers. And third, it offered
reporters plenty of human-interest angles to report on – interviews with servicemen whose families were waiting breathlessly
at home were good for newspaper sales.

There is no doubt that the government realized the value of
'human interest' stories in ensuring favourable coverage of the

H-bomb tests. The Ministry of Supply's own handbook on the tests describes with satisfaction the good publicity created by a scheme linking up men in Christmas Island with children's hospitals in London:

'Towards the end of 1956 [the first H-bomb test took place in May 1957], the various welfare committees in the Operation Area put forward a scheme whereby, at Christmas-time, the men on the island should each give a small Christmas present to a child back home in Great Britain, between the ages of 3 and 8, who was either sick or in some way needy,' it records.

'At the "Grapple" [the code name for the H-bomb tests] headquarters in London, arrangements were made for a large toy firm to supply the toys. Special "Christmas" labels were then sent out to the area, and the soldiers, sailors and airmen wrote out their own individual labels. The toys were sent to the various hospitals and the labels attached. Altogether, 1,967 gifts were distributed.

'Newsreel shots of the toys being distributed at St Mary's Hospital for Women and Children, Plaistow, London, were shown in cinemas throughout the country and photographs were included in the *Daily Telegraph*, *Daily Mirror* and *Daily Sketch*. Further, on Christmas Day, BBC sound and BBC television visited St Stephen's Hospital in Fulham Road and items appeared on "Television News" and on sound "Radio Newsreel" on that day.'

Journalists who were invited to attend one or other of the H-bomb tests were made to feel they were part of a select few who had been chosen to take part in a top secret exercise. The cloak-and-dagger aspect was emphasized in the official invitations sent by the Ministry of Supply. This letter went to William Connor, the *Daily Mirror*'s Cassandra: 'Necessarily this offer is made on the understanding that no indication will be published of when the representatives concerned left this country for this purpose, of when they are due elsewhere to join the necessary transport that will be provided for them, nor of when they leave for the test area.

'For the confidential information of yourself and editors, those who wish to accept this invitation will be required to get themselves to Honolulu by a date which will be given to them. Every effort will be made to make the margin of time between their arrival and departure thence as brief as possible.' The Ministry thoughtfully attached 'some advice on clothing', which suggested the whole affair was going to be like a rather smart party. 'No special protective clothing is required,' it explained, but 'it is suggested that observers should take with them a change of clothing for evening wear.' The tone of the invitation was much more James Bond than anything remotely connected to the dreadful suffering of Hiroshima.

For the most part, it paid off. 'Make no mistake, Britain's H-bomb was a success,' the *Daily Mail* reported on 3 June 1957. Its journalist, John Starr, had been seized by 'the sort of feeling you got in the war after a great victory'. Scientists had assured him that all the fallout had gone to 'ultra-high levels of the atmosphere'. Reassured by what the scientists said, Starr and his colleagues allowed 'raindrops to settle on our exposed skin'.

Another paper printed a letter home from National Serviceman Dave Neyland, an RAF senior aircraftman, which reveals an extraordinary mixture of awe and braggadocio. 'Dear Mum and Dad,' it begins. 'Well, I suppose it's old stuff to you now that they've dropped the rotten thing. Last Monday at approximately 10.15 I saw my first (and I hope it's my last) H-bomb. We worked from 6 o'clock Sunday morning through till 1.30 p.m. Monday without a wink. *I nearly slept right through the whole affair.*'

The text reads suspiciously like a London sub-editor's idea of what a letter home from a working-class lad – Neyland was from Tottenham – would sound like. '"Here is an important announcement" were the words that roused me from dreams of Paris in August..,' it carries on unconvincingly. After the explosion, an officer 'asked me what I thought about the bomb. He said: "You've seen one – you've seen them all!"'' The phlegm of the British serviceman always makes good copy.

There were one or two cautious notes. Cassandra called Britain's second H-bomb test 'a dress rehearsal for the death of the world'. The roar of the hydrogen bomb was, he wrote, 'a source of wonderment and, indeed, of pride to some people', including

Churchill's top scientific adviser, Lord Cherwell. 'But, when released over cities where it would obliterate millions of men, women and children in a trice, it is a wicked, an evil thing.'

The Japanese understandably shared Cassandra's sense of horror. Nor were they convinced by British claims about the cleanness – or lack of fallout – from their bombs. The *Daily Worker* was one of the few papers to report complaints from Japan: 'A Japanese scientist announced in Tokyo yesterday that he had detected radioactive fallout over Japan from Britain's first hydrogen-bomb test at Christmas Island,' it announced on 12 June 1957. Dr Yasuo Miyake, it said, had claimed that his findings disproved Britain's claim about a 'clean' bomb.

But British reporters on the spot were far from critical. 'Scientists and soldiers of Britain's hydrogen-bomb task force are already living and eating normally on Malden Island,' the *Daily Telegraph* reported cheerfully on 3 June. 'This tiny coral atoll was only a few miles in horizontal distance from the point where Friday's multi-megaton bomb went off.'

Where details were lacking, pictures came into their own. As well as mushroom cloud after mushroom cloud, newspapers printed photographs of the men out there, and their wives and families back home. The grinning face of Lieutenant-Commander Jerry Bricker appeared in the *Daily Mail* under the headline, 'The First Man In', explaining how he took off in a helicopter for Malden Island – over which the bomb had exploded – only thirty minutes after one of the tests. 'Security forbade 35-year-old Bricker from describing what the atoll looked like, and what happened to the animals on the island,' the story ran. To make up for this disappointment, the *Mail* printed 'Yesterday's picture of Mrs Bricker with their son and daughter at home at Cranwilliam Road, Lee-on-Solent.'

To judge from the propaganda, in fact, bomb tests seem to have been one jolly family occasion. 'The Misses Billie and Mary Burgess of the Women's Voluntary Services have brought a touch of home to the camp,' the Ministry of Supply booklet on the Grapple Operation reported. 'They are to be found in the main camp NAAFI organizing games, dancing, Highland dancing and concerts, and generally helping to make off-duty hours in the recreation room pleasant and free from boredom.'

The *Mid-Pacific News* SPECIAL SOUVENIR EDITION, printed rather tattily for the servicemen at Christmas Island, contains a curious blend of militaristic boasting with homely details of the men running the test. 'BOMB GONE!' screams its front-page headline. 'H-BOMB PUTS BRITAIN ON LEVEL TERMS.'

'A flash, stark and blinding, high in the Pacific sky, signalled to the world today Britain's emergence as a top-ranking power in this nuclear age,' it declared. 'No one saw it! No human eye could survive the hellish glare of white-hot heat brought to incandescence by the fantastic heat. But those who were present on this historic occasion, backs turned to the explosion nearly thirty miles away, could sense the brilliant intensity of the flash through closed eyelids. Even through thick clothing, a flush of warmth penetrated to the body.'

There is no need to be alarmed, however. The H-bomb test is being run by very English family chaps like Air Vice-Marshal W. E. Oulton, CBE, DSO, DFC, Task Force Commander, whose interests include 'his family, music of all sorts, and sport "in a very middle-aged way". He lives now at Rickmansworth with his family, and his eldest son is in the RAF – at Cranwell.' And like the Scientific Director, the apple-cheeked Mr W. R. J. Cook, MSc, whose face appears in a line drawing below that of Oulton, and who 'lives with his wife and two children at Newbury. Interests? He has none – except his work!'

Servicemen were provided with specially printed envelopes in which to write to the folks back home – the left-hand side is taken up with a stylized mushroom cloud rising over a small coral island. They were even given special cans of beer – the drink and its packaging seems to have occupied an inordinate amount of time in the planning of the British tests – which bore the legend 'SPECIALLY CANNED FOR MEGATON TRIALS' on the top.

The success of Britain's H-bomb tests gave journalists a chance to show off to the Americans, with more than a touch of getting their own back for the way the US had held back from cooperation after the war. 'US defence chiefs were extremely curious to know how the British weapons work when I visited Washington last week,' reported globe-trotting *Daily Express* science reporter, Chapman Pincher, in June 1957.

'Because of the ban on interchange of atomic weapon secrets imposed by the US Government, Sir William Penney has been unable to reveal to the Americans the novel devices which detonate the weapon. While visiting Washington two years ago, Sir William was aghast at the line the Americans were taking, because he had already abandoned it in favour of another method which has been used in the more effective and much cheaper British bombs.

'The British success has been achieved at "shoestring" costs compared with the US methods. The only big special installation involved is at Capenhurst, Cheshire. The US has several enormous plants.

'The success of Operation Grapple – code name for the tests – means that Britain is now independent of America for military might.' One wonders why the phrase 'yah boo, sucks to you' does not actually appear in this panegyric to the British H-bomb tests. Pincher also takes the opportunity to explain that the test series is now over not 'for political reasons or because of any effect of world opinion against H-bomb tests.'

God forbid that any old nonsense like world opinion should interfere with Britain's right to nuclear tests. In fact, Pincher reveals alarmingly, 'the Prime Minister, Mr Harold Macmillan, gave Sir William Penney carte blanche to explode as many H-bombs as were needed to ensure that Britain could stockpile effective deterrent weapons.' The series of tests had ended only because the most recent explosion was a complete success – 'probably the most powerful weapon which has ever been dropped from an airplane' and 'a great advance over any hydrogen weapon possessed by the Americans'.

The British government was lucky to have such devoted servants in the press: privately, both the British and US governments were worried to death in case their electorates found out what the effects of these bombs would be if used in war. It was these fears which were behind the most sinister feature of British propaganda in favour of the nuclear weapons tests – the witch-hunting of anyone who dared to oppose them.

As early as 1954, long before Britain had its own hydrogen bomb, the British government knew that the effect of fallout on the civilian population would be 'bleak'. Cabinet papers from the period show that the Conservative government was terrified that this fact would provoke a public outcry against having the H-bomb if it got out. The result was direct interference with the BBC, which was planning to make a programme on the effects of thermo-nuclear weapons.

In December 1954, the Cabinet had before it a top-secret memorandum written by the then Minister of Defence, Harold Macmillan. In it, Macmillan warned that 'much of the present indifference of the public would vanish' if they discovered that the government was having to alter radically its civil defence plans to cope with the terrible devastation which would be caused by an attack with a single H-bomb.

Macmillan wrote the memorandum after studying the very first assessment by British scientists of the effect of fallout from a ten-megaton bomb – the equivalent of ten million tons of TNT. British scientists had put together the assessment from 'all that we have been able to find out about the effects of the experiments by the United States in the Pacific and elsewhere.' The memo, and the accompanying assessment, make clear that the government was well aware even before Britain had the H-bomb that the effects of nuclear war would be much worse than those subsequently described in its own civil defence propaganda.

'There will be an inner zone of approximately 270 square miles in area (larger than Middlesex), in which radiation will be so powerful that all life will be extinguished, whether in the open or in houses,' the scientists' report predicts. 'Because of the persistence of the radioactive contamination of this inner zone, general relief measures would be virtually impossible for some weeks, and possibly months.'

People in 'specially deep shelters' in this area, with supplies of uncontaminated food and water, would have some chance of survival, 'provided they were not entombed by other effects of the explosion'. Outside this central zone, there would be an area of about 3,000 square miles (several counties wide) in which 'exposure on the first day might easily be fatal'. The report notes that 'no medical means of curing or even curbing the effects of radiation on human beings are yet known'. In the Marshall Islands, it goes on, 'natives on an atoll 110 miles from the explosion received about one-third of the lethal dose.'

The scientists' report raises the possibility of evacuating people in the direct path of fallout in the immediate aftermath of the explosion, since 'fallout will not occur until 8–24 hours after the burst' – a proposal directly ruled out in later government advice on how to survive the bomb. A film made by the Central Office of Information, for example, tells people to do quite the opposite: 'No place in the UK is safer than anywhere else,' it insists. 'No one can tell you where the safest place will be.'

Macmillan's covering memorandum to the Cabinet points out that the new facts about fallout 'must have a revolutionary effect' on the government's preparations for civil defence. 'Thought is already being given to its implications by the limited circle of Ministers and officials to whom this scientific appreciation is known,' he wrote. But he asked the Cabinet to consider a difficult problem. If those responsible for civil defence were allowed to have the information they needed to revise their plans to take account of fallout, 'we must accept some risk that people may come to know quite soon that the Government are planning on this new hypothesis.'

Since this revelation of the horrors the government was anticipating might destroy the public's present 'indifference' to Britain's possession of nuclear weapons, he called for guidance from the Cabinet on how much to tell government departments concerned with defence, and 'the manner in which the implications of fallout for our defence policy should be presented to the public.'

The memo was written at a crucial time for Britain's own nuclear weapons programme. Britain had by now tested three atom bombs in Australia, was hoping to set up a permanent site for testing atom bombs at Maralinga, and had already taken the decision to make its own hydrogen bomb. The last thing the government wanted was a public outcry against British nuclear weapons, sparked off by fear of what would happen to the civilian population in a nuclear war.

The Cabinet had already been made aware of this problem earlier in 1954. A note prepared for a Cabinet committee in May on the effects of nuclear weapons said that, 'if information about these effects is to be published, the manner of its presentation will need to be carefully considered, because not only is the man in the street apt to be more fearful about comparatively mysterious forces like radioactivity than he is about the immediate effects of bomb damage, but also he will be confused by conflicting scientific opinions.'

Now that the first major assessment of these effects had been placed before them, the Cabinet was faced with deciding what to do. One of Macmillan's suggestions, in his covering memo, was an approach to the Americans, who naturally had exactly the same problem – 'there are indications that the United States Government are now considering the political implications of the hydrogen bomb for their home front.' (Indeed they were. Eisenhower had already thrown out an assessment of the dangers of the arms race written by his chief speechwriter, saying: 'We don't want to scare the country to death.')

At the time of writing, the exact decisions taken by the Cabinet after reading Macmillan's memo have not yet been released for public consumption under the thirty-year rule which keeps Cabinet papers secret for that length of time. Their tenor can be gauged, however, not only by the anodyne nature of later civil defence advice issued by successive governments – such as the 'Protect and Survive' booklet – but by a short discussion at a Cabinet meeting late in December 1954.

At that meeting, the Cabinet noted Macmillan's memo and went on to discuss the BBC's plans to produce a programme on the hydrogen bomb early in 1955. The chairman of the Atomic Energy Authority, then Sir Edwin Plowden, had spoken about this project to the Director-General of the BBC, Sir Ian Jacob, the Cabinet minutes record. Sir Ian 'had undertaken to make himself personally responsible for ensuring that those planning the programme consulted *reputable* scientists' (my italics). He had also given an assurance that the programme would be 'free of any political bias'.

The Cabinet was asked to consider whether this matter could now be left to the 'discretion' of the Director-General. They decided not to take any chances. It was important that 'the Government should themselves retain control over the form and timing of publicity on the effects of thermo-nuclear weapons,' the minutes record. They decided that no less a personage than the Prime Minister, Winston Churchill, would arrange for 'further guidance' to be given to the BBC on how to deal with the subject in radio and television programmes.

It is against this background that later developments, such as the banning of Peter Watkins's film, *The War Game*, must be set. At the time that that decision was announced, in November 1965, the BBC's then Director-General, Sir Hugh Greene, said it had been taken simply because the film was too horrifying. It had not been taken 'as a result of outside pressure of any kind'.

The decision is all the more shocking because it was taken under Greene, the most liberal Director-General of the BBC to date. But the BBC *had* come under pressure. It was exercised in that traditionally English way which capitalizes on the fact that there are always people in the right places with the right connections: Lord Normanbrook, chairman of the BBC's governors and a former Cabinet secretary, passed on the message that the government would like the film kept off television screens. It was.

This, then, was the climate in which opposition to the bomb, and to the testing of it, had to operate. With the British government secretly discussing how best to control and restrict the flow of information on the effects of nuclear weapons, it is not surprising that critics of government policy should have found themselves the target of virulent personal abuse.

Opposition to the British bomb tests grew steadily during the 1950s. In 1956, there were protest marches in the Australian city of Perth, where people carried placards complaining they were being used as 'guinea pigs' for the atom bomb tests. In February

1957, an Australian public-opinion poll showed that 66 per cent of the population wanted atom bomb tests banned by international agreement. In April, as Britain got ready to test its first hydrogen bomb at Christmas Island, a poll showed that more Australians were *against* the test than for it – 45 per cent opposed it, with 43 per cent in favour (interestingly, women were three to two against).

The situation was judged sufficiently serious for the Australian government to ask Penney to speak on Australian radio with assurances that the tests had not harmed anyone. Penney was asked about this broadcast when he gave evidence to the Australian Royal Commission in London in 1985. The questioning was done by Peter McClellan, the Sydney barrister assisting the commission. The exchanges between the two men are revealing.

First, Penney was asked whether he took any steps to check the reliability of the methods used to collect data about fallout on the Australian mainland – data on which he based his assurances to the Australian public.

PENNEY No. I was shown values... Here was some fallout. I think it was given to me by the Australians... They were made by competent physicists.

In fact, there were deficiencies in the methods used to monitor fallout, which Penney himself admitted under questioning. But on the basis of the figures given to him, he made a radio broadcast assuring the Australians there would be no harmful consequences from the tests. He was then asked about hostile public opinion, which was the reason why he had been invited to speak on Australian radio.

MCCLELLAN Did you ever feel concern ... at that stage ... that there was any real prospect ... by reason of the reaction of the Australian public ... it might come to an end?
PENNEY No I didn't. In fact, I'm slightly surprised [to hear] there was a hostile reaction.

The commission was later told that Penney had complained in a letter about 'cranks in Australia equipped with Geiger

93

counters waiting for radioactive rain'. For the moment, McClellan simply put the opinion-poll results cited above to him.

PENNEY What I ... on a similar theme ... I do remember going to Canberra, I can't tell you whether it was after Buffalo or Totem [series of tests which took place in 1956 and 1953, respectively]. I talked to Dr Evatt [the Leader of the Opposition] who said, 'I don't agree with what you're doing, I think it's terrible.' I said, 'I don't like it much, but I think we're going to stop war that way.' We had a long discussion. That was the kind of position ... I was very well aware *he and many in the Labour party who supported him* didn't like it *but that was not quite the same.* (My italics.)

Poor old Dr Evatt. He was only the elected leader of the opposition, so why should anyone take any notice of him? This was certainly a view shared by Chapman Pincher, who wrote in 1957: 'Dr Herbert Evatt, the consistently pro-Russian leader of the Australian Left-wing opposition, surprised nobody when he jumped on the ban-the-British-bomb bandwagon.'

Britain often congratulates itself for not having instituted McCarthyite witch-hunts in the 1950s. But the terms of abuse applied to opponents of the bomb tests by British journalists, scientists and politicians bear all the hallmarks of just such a campaign. It was a crude attempt to silence opposition by the use of smear tactics.

The method was straightforward. It worked on the unspoken suggestion that because, according to its protagonists, there were no real arguments against possessing and testing the bomb, opposition to it must be political. Who would benefit if Britain did not have the bomb? The answer was Russia. Therefore anyone who criticized the bomb tests must, at least secretly, be a pro-Russian communist. This is a clever, if crude, tactic, because it diverts attention away from the many real political and, even more importantly, *scientific* arguments against the tests. Chapman Pincher's writing on this subject provides an interesting example of the media's response.

Pincher is a journalist who writes for the *Daily Express*. In his writings about the bomb in the 1940s and 1950s, he got key things wrong. On one occasion, as he later admitted, his story was based on guess work rather than fact. Linus Pauling is an American chemist. He is the only scientist, apart from Marie Curie, to win the Nobel Prize twice. By 1957, when Britain was about to test its first H-bomb, he was a dedicated campaigner against weapons tests because of their effect on the atmosphere. He predicted that 1,000 people would die if Britain went ahead with its first H-bomb test in the Pacific Ocean.

On 1 May, 1957, Chapman Pincher went on the attack in the *Daily Express*. 'Here it comes again,' he began wearily. 'Read it above – this monstrous charge by a top-ranking scientist that the British are about to murder 1,000 people by testing an H-bomb.

'Fortunately, this charge can be ignored, for though brilliant in the laboratory, Dr Linus Pauling is fatuous in politics. (The US Government had to refuse him permission to leave the country for many months.)'

Note the masterly use of the damning parenthesis. Why would the US government have to forbid Pauling to leave the country? Because he is a suspected traitor? Pincher doesn't even need to say it. But Pincher does produce a reason for the opposition of Pauling and a growing number of other scientists and politicians to the British tests to divert attention away from the dangerous territory of scientific argument.

'Why has Britain's proposal to explode an H-bomb in an entirely uninhabited part of the Pacific provoked such hysterical and sustained opposition throughout the world?' he goes on. 'I will tell you. Because through a peculiar set of circumstances, the test provides those who hate or envy the British with an extraordinary opportunity to injure them.'

Who are these horrid people? Pincher has the answer to hand in the form of a crudely racist and anti-communist litany. There are 'Jap business tycoons' who are 'already using underhand methods to beat Britain in the export markets'. There is the Indian Prime Minister, Mr Nehru – 'pretending that Asia is seriously threatened by radioactive fallout from a British bomb is an effective way of fomenting nationalism among ignorant people.'

Nor is there any need to wonder why 'the Socialist supporters of Mr Aneurin Bevan are manipulating the H-test issue to weaken Mr Hugh Gaitskell's hold on the party leadership.

'Of course, not all the opposition is deliberately political. There are always a few highly vocal individuals who seize on such an opportunity to give publicity to their own fanciful fears and fads.

'Thus making common cause with the Communists on this issue, there is Bertrand Russell, who opposes the test on moral grounds. There is Dr Albert Schweitzer, who, having deliberately sealed himself off from the realities of politics, sends up a cry from the African swamps that the H-test must be banned on medical grounds.'

So far, the opposition is made up of out-and-out communists and those naïve enough to play into their hands. What about the scientists? They are just as bad. 'Some, like Dr Pauling and Polish-born Professor Joseph Rotblat' – he must be suspect if he's Polish, even though he left before the outbreak of the Second World War – 'of St Bartholomew's Hospital, warn of radioactive dangers to a degree not supported by eminent experts advising the Government.

'Others, like Professor Christopher Powell, of Bristol, and Professor Joliot Curie, of Paris, speak on behalf of the World Federation of Scientific Workers, an organization so riddled with Communists that it has been forbidden to meet in Britain.

'Finally, there are the pacifists, opposed to weapons of every kind and dedicated to the principle that it is always better to live on your knees than die on your feet.' What these people are doing, says Pincher, is chanting, 'Woe, woe, with a harmony which is marvellously melodious to the Kremlin's ears.'

This article is ostensibly about a specific claim by an eminent scientist about the medical effects of an H-bomb test. What is lacking in it is any discussion of that claim other than one throwaway phrase – the allegation that Pauling and Rotblat warn of 'radioactive dangers to a degree not supported by eminent experts advising the Government'.

Who are these advisers? How would they answer Pauling's very specific claim about the effect of the test? The whole point

of the piece is to divert attention away from this scientific controversy, in which the opponents of the test can muster just as
impressive a set of experts as can the government, to unsubstantiated innuendoes about anyone who doesn't support the British
government's line.

What about Pincher's own credentials? He is the journalist
who told us that the first British atom bomb 'was almost certainly exploded on the top of a steel tower' when it was actually
inside HMS *Plym*. He is the journalist who published a book
called *Into the Atomic Age* by 'Chapman Pincher, BSc' in 1948,
in which he described how the uranium gun bomb was tested at
Alamogordo. It was not. As we have seen, scientists were confident the uranium bomb, Little Boy, would work. What they
tried out was the plutonium implosion bomb, Fat Man.

On 19 March 1957 Pincher said in a story in the *Daily Express*
that Britain intended to run a further series of atom bomb tests
at Maralinga that year; most would be exploded on top of
towers, but one might be dropped from a plane.

When the British government started looking for the source of
the leak, Pincher sent a letter explaining the origin of the story.
It had come from Australia, he said, and his source said the
series would finish work started at an earlier set of tests. That,
he said, was why 'I suggested most of the weapons would be
tower bursts and that one might be dropped from an airplane.
This I confess was *sheer guess-work* based on what happened in
the previous series . . . The fact is that if my guess about what is
going to happen in these new trials is correct, *it was something of
a fluke.*' (My italics.)

Pincher, of course, was not alone in the practice of dismissing
opposition to the tests. *The Times* of 18 May 1957 reported a stu-
dent demonstration at the British embassy in Tokyo to protest
against a British H-bomb tests. The students' federation was 'a
notoriously fellow-travelling organization, and today's protest
march showed all the signs of careful planning and forethought,'
the story said. Even the poor old Japanese were not allowed to
have a legitimate interest in the effects of radiation.

That thoughtful journal, the *News of the World*, made its contribution to the debate by inviting Lord Cherwell, Churchill's

wartime scientific adviser, to make a statement on Britain's first H-bomb. 'Until today he, as well as other top-flight scientists, has kept silent on the effects of Britain's H-bomb tests in the Pacific,' the paper reported on 19 May 1957. 'Now for the first time Lord Cherwell answers some of the questions which are disturbing people all over the world today.

'Lord Cherwell – he is known as "The Prof" to Sir Winston – sat back in his armchair as I read the statement. " I accept your paper's invitation because I think it vital the truth should be known," said the tall, lean man in tweeds who knows all Britain's scientific secrets – and has done for years.'

Given what he goes on to say, it is hard to see why Cherwell's views had been kept a secret for so long. Under the heading 'UNANSWERABLE FACTS', Cherwell begins uncompromisingly. 'Many people in this country and abroad have been genuinely worried about the alleged danger to the health of the world caused by our nuclear tests in the Pacific. Their anxiety is completely unfounded.'

Their anxiety had been stirred up, in fact, by a curious group of people identified by Cherwell as 'freelances' – the implication being that their opposition, far from being genuine, had been paid for by the highest bidder. These people, whom Cherwell goes on to traduce as 'agitators', had claimed the bomb tests must be stopped in spite of a report from the Medical Research Council which 'gave us facts and figures showing that these tests will not harm any of us'.

This assertion, impressive as it sounds, is merely Cherwell up to his old tricks again. During the Second World War, as Frederick Lindemann, Cherwell distorted scientific evidence to persuade Churchill to lift his embargo on area bombing. In 1957, he was simply misrepresenting a cautious report by the MRC which had admitted the possibility that even low doses of radiation could cause cancer. But were the readers of the *News of the World* in any position to argue with 'The Prof'?

In the face of this stream of sustained and abusive propaganda, it is remarkable that the voice of dissent succeeded in being heard at all. It certainly found little outlet in the popular press, which was besotted with the bomb as the restorer of the nation's virility.

It did surface in publications from scientific organizations. Linus Pauling based his claim that 1,000 people would die as a result of Britain's first H-bomb test on a report from the Atomic Scientists' Association in April 1957. The Association, based in Britain, had set up a committee to follow up problems raised in the MRC report the previous year. It was chaired by Joseph Rotblat.

It recognized the problem that the effects of small amounts of radiation were simply not known. But it suggested that an H-bomb of the type tested by the US at Bikini in 1954 'may eventually produce bone cancers in 1,000 people for every million tons of TNT or equivalent explosive'. No wonder Chapman Pincher was reluctant to get involved in the turbulent scientific debate about the effects of the test; it was much safer to stick to unsubstantiated innuendo.

Dissent also appeared in journals with comparatively small circulations. Of these, the *New Statesman* played a key role. In 1952, its 'London Diary' was one of the few voices to call attention to the outbreak of lunacy spreading through Fleet Street.

'A great deal of nonsense is being written about the A-bomb explosion at Monte Bello,' it pointed out. '"Now Great Britain is really Great again," exclaimed the *Evening Standard*, and other leader writers patted us on the back with much the same heartiness. Yet the fact is that no one in London or Washington can possibly know whether our bomb is more effective than the American bomb, since each has been produced secretly. What the leader writers mean, I suppose, is that it takes a Great Power to make A-bombs and that now we're making them we can hold up our heads alongside the Russians and Americans.'

In 1957, the *Statesman*'s 'London Diary' reported incredulously that Lady Carew Pole, organizer of the WVS in Cornwall, had written to all her branches saying, 'The hydrogen bomb could be a terrible weapon, but with your help the blow can be greatly eased.' She urged women to attend talks on how to protect their homes, how to care for the sick at home, and 'how you would be cared for'. Kingsley Martin, the paper's editor, commented, 'I have long suspected that the government's purpose in keeping civil defence organizations going was more psychological than practical.'

On 2 November 1957, the *New Statesman* published an article by J. B. Priestley, 'Britain and the Nuclear Bombs', which called for Britain to reject nuclear weapons. 'Alone, we defied Hitler; and alone we can defy this nuclear madness into which the spirit of Hitler seems to have passed, to poison the world,' he wrote. 'There may be other chain reactions besides those leading to destruction; and we might start one.' He urged 'a declaration to the world that after a certain date one power able to engage in nuclear warfare will reject the evil thing forever.'

The article was published just after the Labour Party conference had rejected a motion that Britain should disarm unilaterally; it provoked a great debate and led to the setting up of the Campaign for Nuclear Disarmament. The first meeting was attended by Kingsley Martin, the paper's editor, and Patrick Blackett, the Nobel Prize-winning physicist whose advice against the bomb had been peremptorily rejected by Ernest Bevin.

The aims of CND have still not been realized; nevertheless, the tide was turning against the bomb tests. By 1963, opposition to them was so strong that Britain, Russia and the US signed the Partial Test Ban Treaty which outlawed tests in the atmosphere. The problems are not over: France and China have ignored the treaty, radiation has escaped from underground tests into the air, and radioactivity from the 1950s' tests is making its way back to earth to this day. But at least the days of large, uncontrolled emissions of radiation into the atmosphere, unless there is a nuclear war, are over.

Curiously, the attitudes that went with them still persist. They even find publishers who are willing to print them. Air Vice-Marshal Stewart Menaul, a high-ranking Royal Air Force officer during British tests at Maralinga and at the later tests at Monte Bello, is a case in point.

In 1980, Menaul published a book called *Countdown: Britain's Strategic Nuclear Forces*. The book jacket claims that, in it, Menaul tells for the first time the 'whole story' of how Britain designed and tested nuclear weapons.

Menaul's style is one with which students of 1950s' propaganda have become familiar. 'The Labour Government, elected in 1945, had among its members an assortment of Communist fellow-travellers, conscientious objectors and pacifists whom Ernest Bevin, the Foreign Secretary, distrusted implicitly, though Attlee tolerated them,' Menaul says. In the circumstances, he feels, it was quite right that decisions about the British bomb should have been taken without reference to the full Cabinet, or to Parliament. 'In retrospect, to anyone who has been involved in nuclear affairs in the post-war era, the manner in which decisions were taken by Gen 163 was entirely correct and appropriate.'

He allows that 'some government scientific advisers, like Professor P. M. Blackett, opposed Britain's nuclear programme, but his views carried little weight *except among his own kind.* Professor Lindemann (later Viscount Cherwell), who was Churchill's principal scientific adviser, had no doubts and fully supported the programme right up to the final test phases in Australia and at Christmas Island.' (My italics.)

Menaul believes the British tests harmed no one. How reliable this view is can be gauged from what he says about the American nuclear tests. The tests in Nevada in 1955, he says, 'provided visitors and local inhabitants with a spectacular and interesting display to distract their attention from the more fleshy entertainments to be had in the enchanting city of Las Vegas.' Fortunately, he goes on to explain, they were conducted – just like the British tests – under regulations 'designed to protect life and property from the effects of nuclear weapons and make testing on the American mainland *safe and effective.*' (My italics.)

In its issue of 13 January 1984, the *Journal of the American Medical Association* printed a paper on the incidence of cancer 'in an Area of Radioactive Fallout Downwind From the Nevada Test Site'. Its author, Carl J. Johnson, reports five times as many cases of leukaemia as would have been expected in the period between 1958 and 1966. The excess persisted in the later period studied, 1972 to 1980. There were also excess cases of thyroid cancer – which is caused by radioactive iodine – and of breast cancer.

'There were more cancers of the gastrointestinal tract than expected,' the paper says. 'There was an excess of melanoma, bone cancer and brain tumours. A subgroup with a history of acute fallout effects had a higher cancer incidence. That these cases can be associated with radiation exposures is supported by a comparison between groups of the ratio of cancers of more radiosensitive organs with all other types of cancer.'

The paper, which was published only after very careful independent scrutiny of its methodology and results, is hardly a tribute to the 'safety' of the American mainland tests. But Menaul is very good at looking on the bright side. Later in his book, he recognizes the hazards caused by the US tests at Bikini in 1954 – when numerous Pacific islanders got high doses of radiation – but goes on to say that 'in fairness to the Americans, it must be said that valuable information resulting from their tests was made known to the world by the American Atomic Energy Authority.'

Attendance at the British bomb tests was, as far as Menaul was concerned, a privilege. 'Those who were lucky enough to have taken part in these historic events had a unique experience and a greater understanding of the importance of nuclear deterrence in maintaining world peace,' he writes at the end of a chapter on the British tests. His book is dedicated to 'the men and women of all three Services who loyally carry out their duties despite scant recognition from their political masters, and all too often in the face of ill-informed criticism from a small but vocal minority who appear to owe allegiance to authorities beyond our shores.'

CHAPTER FIVE

'Hairy-chested' attitudes

Comment from declassified US document
on officers' approach to radiation risks

During the 1950s, opposition to the atom bomb and H-bomb tests focused on one specific medical issue: the claim that fallout from tests conducted in the atmosphere posed a threat to people throughout the world. On one side of the argument were ranged people like Edward Teller, who was known as the father of the American hydrogen bomb, and Lord Cherwell; on the other, an alliance of scientists embracing Linus Pauling in the US and Andrei Sakharov in Russia.

Teller claimed world-wide fallout 'is as dangerous as being an ounce overweight or smoking one cigarette every two months'. Sakharov claimed the victims of fallout had already, by 1958, reached almost one million and would rise by up to 300,000 more for every year the testing continued. Cherwell simply thundered that the tests would harm no one.

Today, few people would take Cherwell's position. Even the conservative Nuclear Regulatory Commission in Washington recognizes some damage. In 1979, Robert E. Alexander, of its Office of Standards Development, estimated the long-term effects of atmospheric weapons testing at between 29,000 and 72,000 deaths from cancer and 168,000 genetic effects. Dr Rosalie Bertell, an American radiation expert, claims the production and testing of nuclear weapons up to 1984 had already killed or damaged 13 million people.

But even if pessimistic estimates are correct, the effects are difficult to measure when spread across the population of the world, with all the problems of discrepancies in the efficiency of diagnosis and registration of disease in different countries. The effects are much more likely to show up – in the form of a higher-than-predicted incidence of radiation-linked diseases – in a relatively small population known to have been close to one or more nuclear explosions.

The bomb test veterans – servicemen and civilians who took part in the British tests – are just such a population. It is clear that, at the time of the tests, few of the men themselves recognized the risk. They gave the matter little thought, or trusted to the superior knowledge of the people running the tests. The other group of people who were at risk, the aboriginal population of Australia, was even less in a position to realize the danger or do anything about it.

Britain's last atom bomb tests took place in Australia in 1957, its final H-bomb test in the Pacific in 1958. That year, Britain, the USSR and the US agreed to a voluntary suspension of tests in the atmosphere. The agreement broke down in 1961, but Britain did not resume atmospheric testing of full-scale weapons. In 1963, the Partial Test Ban Treaty came into effect. That year also marked the last in a series of experiments, running into hundreds, which Britain conducted in Australia in connection with the nuclear weapons programme.

1963 did not bring with it the end of Britain's involvement with the testing range at Maralinga, in the South Australian desert. In 1967, when the tests had become a closed chapter in history for most people in the UK, the British were hauled back to Australia to clear up the mess they had left behind at Maralinga, including at least twenty kilograms of plutonium and traces of beryllium, a highly toxic substance. That exercise, code-named Operation Brumby and described in a key secret document known as the Pearce Report, was to play a vital role in the fight for a full investigation into what happened at the tests when the first allegations of illness were made years later.

Many radiation-linked diseases take years to develop. In the 1970s, veterans in Britain and Australia began to suspect that a surprising number of them were suffering from diseases like cancer, cataracts and skin diseases. Events followed a similar pattern in both countries, although the campaign started later in Britain. In the US, the same thing was happening: former US servicemen who had taken part in tests at Nevada and in the

Pacific, as well as those who visited the devastated cities of Hiroshima and Nagasaki, noticed high levels of disease and linked them with their experience. In the Pacific, islanders who had suffered years of French and American weapons testing started to campaign for compensation for their devastated territory.

The campaigns each began in the same quiet way. Men who were at nuclear tests tried to find out more about their illnesses and the tests themselves, coming up against official denials of any connection, and against the wall of secrecy which surrounds nuclear weapons. They went to the media for help; publicity brought forward more people with similar tales to tell. They formed veterans' associations to fight the particular problems in each country: in the US and Britain, legislation which prevents former servicemen suing the state for injuries received during their service; in Australia, stringent cash limits on the amount of compensation that could be awarded.

They also demanded large-scale, independent surveys of their health to establish whether their claims of high rates of illness were correct. The studies done so far in Australia and the US have been inconclusive, because they missed out some of the participants. In Britain, the government set up a study by the National Radiological Protection Board; it has been fraught with problems, heavily criticized, and is nowhere near its final report at the time of writing. The study will be discussed in more detail in a later chapter.

In Australia, one of the first cases to gain public attention was that of Warrant Officer William Jones, who died of bone cancer in 1966. His widow, Peggy, first started trying to get compensation for herself and her children in 1968, two years after her husband's death. William Jones had served in the Australian army at Emu Field in 1953, during the Totem series of British tests.

He had been told to leave a Centurion tank close to where the weapon was to be detonated; after the explosion, he was sent into the area to bring the tank back. The tank would not start and Jones stayed beside it for two days until spare parts could be brought. He then drove it back to an army base in Victoria.

Jones tried to get compensation before his death but failed. Peggy Jones was finally awarded compensation, under the Compensation (Australian Government Employees) Act, in 1974 – Aust. $8,600 and small weekly payments for each of her four children. Although the award was tiny, the important point was that the Commissioner for Employees' Compensation who heard the case decided that Jones had contracted his illness because of the nature of his employment with the army.

In 1980, Lance Edwards, a former RAAF radio operator, went on Australian television to describe how he had become contaminated flying through the atomic cloud at Emu Field in 1953. Edwards's story of how he had to shower thirteen times to get rid of the contamination was alarming, but no one knew at that time just how badly contaminated the Lincolns had been – it would not become clear until the publication of a damning Australian report on the tests, the Kerr Report, in 1984.

Nevertheless, Edwards's illness – cancer of the thyroid, an organ known to be sensitive to radiation – was accepted by the Australian government as a 'disease due to the nature of his employment', just as William Jones's cancer had been. Edwards was one of the lucky ones: by 1983, less than a dozen of the hundred or so cases brought under this compensation system had been successful. The largest award was Aust. $30,000. Relying on the Australian courts, rather than the compensation system for workmen, proved no better. The only cases to be won have been brought by widows; no survivor of the tests has yet won a case in court.

The Australian Nuclear Veterans' Association was set up, with headquarters in Brisbane, to coordinate the men's fight. In 1980, it drew up a list of demands; the key items were calls for compensation and a demand for the setting-up of a register of all the people who believed their health had been affected by nuclear weapons. The Conservative government's reaction was to refuse to release names to ANVA for such a register.

Ex-servicemen were not the only people in Australia who were becoming worried about the effects of the tests. In 1980, the council in South Australia which represents aborigines told the Minister for Aboriginal Affairs that some of the

Pitjantjatjara people could have been injured by radiation from the British bombs exploded in South Australia. In particular, an aborigine called Yami Lester described a black mist which passed over Wallatinna Station after an explosion just over 100 miles away at Emu Field in 1953. A number of aborigines became very ill, he said, particularly the very young and very old; he himself later went blind.

The Australian government responded to all these allegations and court cases by asking the Australian Ionising Radiation Advisory Committee to examine the available evidence on the tests. This they did in the report already mentioned, AIRAC 9, which was published in January 1983. Its conclusions were comforting. 'The measures taken to protect the public, and the personnel involved in the nuclear test programs, from radiation injury attributable to the tests were well planned and almost certainly were effective,' it said.

It could not have been published at a worse time. Events were taking place in Britain which would undermine AIRAC's cheerful conclusions to the point where a full-scale Royal Commission would be considered necessary by the Australian government. What was happening in Britain was much the same as had already occurred in Australia, but with this difference: the British government had run the tests, and scraps of documentary evidence were to be found in Britain which were not available in Australia.

Some British veterans began to suspect a connection with the bomb tests as soon as their diseases were diagnosed. At the end of 1982, the BBC's *Nationwide* programme publicized the claims of men who had participated in the hydrogen bomb tests at Christmas Island. In January 1983, Channel Four showed a programme on Maralinga which included footage from an Australian film, *Backs to the Blast*, in which Australian veterans talked about their experience.

I took up the story in the *Sunday Times*, as did David Leigh and Paul Lashmar in the *Observer*. Starting in January 1983, I wrote eight stories in the *Sunday Times* about the veterans. They included the revelation that an Australian responsible for monitoring radiation exposure at Maralinga had admitted that

essential pieces of equipment had failed to work and conse-
quently he had made up records of radiation exposure. Lady
Connor, widow of the *Daily Mirror* columnist, Cassandra, told
the *Sunday Times* she believed her husband's death could be
connected with a hydrogen-bomb test he had observed at
Christmas Island.

The articles attracted many letters; some were from men who
wanted to contact a veterans' organization in Britain, some from
people who just wanted to tell someone about their experiences.
One man wrote from Devon to say how pleased he was that the
claims of the veterans were at last being taken seriously. 'I have
often wondered if any of my ailments over the years had anything to do with the H-bomb test,' he wrote. 'I even asked a
doctor and I was scoffed at.' He described a skin irritation which
started soon after the test, when he was twenty-two, and persisted to the time of writing. 'I used to wear white cotton gloves
when I went to bed but this didn't stop me from scratching my
face and chest until they bled.'

A London woman, who did not want any publicity, wrote to
tell me about her husband's infertility after the Monte Bello test
in 1952. He was a member of a boat party which had been unable
to get back to the parent ship before the test; they pulled in to an
island and watched the test from out in the open. The woman's
husband had asked his consultant whether radiation could have
played a part in his infertility; the doctor took it sufficiently
seriously to write to the Ministry of Defence, which simply
denied any connection.

Almost as soon as the veterans' claims received publicity, the
British government simultaneously denied that anyone had
been harmed and announced it would commission a study into
their health to put people's minds at rest. Although the study
was announced in January, it took eight months to set up and
many veterans were unhappy about the way the Ministry of
Defence intended going about the task. In May 1983, the
veterans set up the British Nuclear Tests' Veterans' Association, under the chairmanship of Ken McGinley, the former
Royal Engineer who lives in Dunoon, in Scotland. It soon had
hundreds of members, including many who had contacted

newspapers, like the *Sunday Times*, or the BBC's *Nationwide* programme.

In Birmingham, Dr Alice Stewart, the well-known epidemiologist, whose work first revealed the cancer-inducing effects of X-rays on the foetus, studied the health of veterans from Christmas Island who had contacted the *Nationwide* programme. Her initial findings, published in the *Lancet* in April 1983, suggested a surprisingly high incidence of deaths from leukaemia and cancer of the lymph glands.

Stewart's letter suggested several possible causes for the excess: that the men were exposed to more radiation than previously thought; that the effects of low-level radiation were more severe than previously thought; or that more men had taken part in the tests than the researchers had allowed for. (Stewart's study involved working out the number of illnesses and deaths which would normally be expected among the group of men who took part, and comparing it to the incidence of illness they had actually suffered.)

Her letter was printed in the *Lancet* above another on the same subject. The second letter was signed by Joseph Rotblat, by now Emeritus Professor of Physics at London University, and six other eminent scientists. It pointed out that, while the excess of cancers shown in Stewart's study might not be related to radiation, it had thrown up another suggestive statistic – ten cases of cataract. 'While ... there may be causes other than radiation for the excess RES malignancies [the cancers already mentioned], the reported incidence of cataract, virtually unknown as a spontaneous occurrence among young men, is a strong indication that some of those involved had received radiation greatly in excess of a safe dose,' it said.

Rotblat and his colleagues called for an independent academic body to be given the job of making a full investigation into 'the morbidity, mortality, and perhaps genetic effects in these men.' As we shall see, this is not what happened. In October, after the government increased its estimate of the number of men who took part in the Christmas Island tests – a possibility that Stewart's letter had already foreseen – Stewart accepted that her original results could not now be relied upon. Although the government could not help crowing about this development, the admission did not give the nuclear tests a clean bill of health. It merely underlined the need for a comprehensive study.

In 1984, two developments took place which were instrumental in persuading the Australian government, if not the British, of the need for a new inquiry. On 11 March, I published in the *Sunday Times* details of a top-secret memorandum which led David Alton, the Liberal MP, to claim servicemen had been used as 'guinea pigs' at the tests. The 1953 memo, which had recently been released to the Public Records Office at Kew, discussed the needs of the various Services at future bomb tests. 'The Army must discover the detailed effects of various types of explosion on equipment, stores and *men with and without protection*,' it commented candidly. (My italics.)

The Ministry of Defence denied that men had deliberately been exposed to radiation, but admitted they had been placed only one-and-a-half miles from a bomb test in the Buffalo series in 1956. The idea was to give them 'some experience' of being close to a nuclear explosion. The story caused a furore and sparked off new calls for an investigation; the next day's Melbourne *Age* led its front page with the *Sunday Times* revelations and reported demands in Australia for an inquiry into ex-servicemen's claims.

A few weeks later, a copy of a still secret document, the Pearce Report on Operation Brumby, was leaked to the *National Times*, an Australian weekly newspaper. It revealed that the minor experiments which went on at Maralinga right up until 1963 had left thousands of acres contaminated with plutonium. They had created it seemed, a worse hazard than the actual weapons tests.

A general election had brought to power the Labour government under Bob Hawke just over a year before. In opposition, Labour had been sympathetic to the complaints of the bomb veterans. Faced with the new revelations, the government decided to act. A week after the *National Times* story about Maralinga appeared, in May, Australia's Energy Minister, Peter Walsh, set up a committee to review data on fallout from the tests. It was headed by Charles Kerr, Professor of Preventive and Social Medicine at the University of Sydney.

The committee's brief was a demanding one: review the evidence and report by the end of the same month. What it produced was a detailed forty-three-page critique of the soothing picture offered the previous year by AIRAC 9: 'The Committee concluded that AIRAC 9 could not be regarded as an authoritative scientific account nor as an informative public record of important aspects of the British nuclear tests.'

The Kerr report recommended the setting up of a Royal Commission to investigate the tests. Although the Labour Prime Minister, Bob Hawke, is not believed to have been over-enthusiastic – his stance on nuclear issues has repeatedly angered many Labour supporters – the government went ahead and announced the Royal Commission in July 1984.

Although its terms of reference direct it to look at the effects of the atom bomb tests on Australians, the development was not one calculated to raise cheers among members of the British government. Since the British had deliberately kept Australia as much in the dark as possible about the tests, any dirty washing hauled out for inspection was likely to belong firmly to Britain.

This fact was reflected in the thoroughly uneasy, often hostile relationship between the British government and the commission. When the commission started its hearings in Australia in autumn 1984, the new British High Commissioner, Sir John Leahy, complained that the public hearings 'reflected on the British government'. The commission's president, Mr Justice James McClelland, a dryly witty former Labour member of the Australian Senate, complained that Britain was tying the commission's hands by allowing it to see declassified documents only if it agreed to keep them secret.

Britain was not represented at the autumn hearings of the commission in Australia. It changed its mind only in time to brief a QC for the London hearings, which started on 3 January 1985. The commission opened in London in a blaze of publicity, part of which was engendered by a public row between the judge and Adam Butler, the junior Defence Minister acting as spokesman for the British government.

Just before Christmas, Butler told the House of Commons: 'I am persuaded by the evidence that I have seen, and from studying the matter as closely as I can, that precautions were adequate and observed.' On the opening day, Judge McClelland hit back. 'At this stage of our investigation, I am unable to say that the evidence which we have received would permit us safely to reach the comfortable conclusion which the Minister has reached,' he said.

Britain had given repeated assurances of its willingness to co-operate, but he went on: 'If I retain some doubt as to the whole-heartedness of these assurances it is because they have not always been matched by conduct that one might have expected to back them up.

'It is only in recent weeks that the British government has decided to be represented before the commission. There are grounds for believing that this decision was taken reluctantly and only after the commission had publicly suggested that the British government was dragging its feet.

'The nuclear tests were carried out by the British and the evidence which has already been adduced suggests to us that they told the Australian authorities almost nothing about what they were doing in Australia during the tests.

'Since the British know so much more than we do about what they did in our country at that time, cooperation now, if it is to mean anything, involves not simply telling us that we are free to delve into the mountain of documents which are in British hands but positive assistance in bringing to light anything of relevance which those documents may disclose.'

McClelland also complained that the British government had agreed to hearings on British soil only if the Australians 'would waive the usual right to initiate punitive proceedings against persons giving perjured evidence.' At the time, this assertion by the judge, widely interpreted as a licence to lie on the part of the British witnesses, went unchallenged by the government. It was denied in rather mystifying circumstances – an article by Adam Butler in the *Guardian* – only after the commission had been sitting for several weeks.

What was behind the judge's speech was a row between the

commission and the British government over access to documents. The British had thirty-eight tons of them, and Peter McClellan, the barrister assisting the commission, wanted to see a lot of them. He also wanted to call as witnesses British scientists who took part in the tests. Up to the time of the commission's arrival in Britain, the British government had been distinctly uncooperative.

The commission did have one card up its sleeve, however. When it was set up, Margaret Thatcher had written to the Australian Prime Minister, Bob Hawke, promising full cooperation. The judge's comments were a calculated reminder of that fact, and they worked. The Attorney-General, Sir Michael Havers, pointed out to members of the British government that the holding back of documents and witnesses could not be maintained. The commission got what it wanted.

Between 3 January and 18 March, British and Australian veterans were able to watch flesh being wrapped around the bones of allegations they had originally made as long as five years before. Some of the revelations were confirmatory. The Totem I test had been fired in the most dangerous possible conditions and was responsible for the 'black mist' which aborigines at Wallatinna Station talked about, for instance. Others were new and startling – among these that Scotland had been seriously considered as the venue for testing the trigger of an atom bomb, along with Skipsea, in Yorkshire, and Donna Nook, an RAF bombing range in Lincolnshire.

By the time the commission was ready to go home and resume taking evidence in Australia, the veterans felt they had been publicly vindicated. The *Guardian* said the hearings had left 'a frightening catalogue of ignorant and careless acts'. Even the deeply conservative *Times* allowed that 'enough evidence has now been extracted from archives and witnesses to undermine the bland and brief reassurances which Britain has issued at regular intervals since the tests'. Adam Butler remained silent.

Even if the British government did not have detailed knowledge of all the documents it held on the atom bomb tests – a likely eventuality, in view of their sheer number – the precedent for declassifying such information was hardly a happy one from the Cabinet's point of view.

In 1979, an American former soldier called Orville Kelly set up the National Association of Atomic Veterans to represent the quarter of a million US personnel who had taken part in nuclear tests or risked exposure to radiation in the bombed cities of Hiroshima and Nagasaki. Kelly was US army commander of Japtan Island, in the Marshall Islands, in 1958; he saw twenty-two bomb tests in only four months. Kelly died of cancer only months after founding the veterans' organization, but his wife, Wanda, carried on its work with other men who had been at the tests.

It had long been known that the US tests in the Pacific had had disastrous consequences for the islanders in whose territory they were held. The huge hydrogen device tested at Bikini Atoll on 1 March 1954 – its yield was equal to 15 million tons of TNT – irradiated the Marshall Islands and in particular Rongelap Atoll, where the inhabitants suffered burns and radiation sickness before they were hurriedly evacuated. Fallout also landed on a Japanese fishing boat, the *Lucky Dragon*; one crew member died of radiation sickness and almost all of the remaining twenty-two showed signs of it.

But, until the spring of 1983, American ex-servicemen had little hard evidence to back up their claims of ill-health because of the tests. In May that year, congressional hearings were held to examine their claims after much campaigning by the veterans' organization, NAAV.

The evidence presented to the congressional hearings was startling. It suggested that 'significant numbers' of the 42,000 US personnel taking part in two atom bomb tests at Bikini Atoll in 1946 'probably received very high doses of radiation in tissue destructive ranges'.

The evidence came from recently declassified papers which had been donated to the library of the University of California, Los Angeles, by Colonel Stafford L. Warren, Chief of the Radiological Safety Section during the tests in 1946. It was presented in the shape of an evaluation of these official, formerly secret documents carried out at the International Radiation Research and Training Institute.

The tests, known as Operation Crossroads, are particularly interesting because the second, 'Baker', was the first ever underwater explosion. One of the people who watched it was William Penney – his observation of the 'base surge' phenomenon persuaded him to make the first British test at Monte Bello an underwater explosion. At 20 kilotons, Baker was slightly smaller than the first British bomb. But it produced a dreadful list of errors and hazards.

The official US position on its bomb tests is identical to that of the British on theirs. 'Exposures generally were well within established radiation exposure limits and there was no reason to expect any increased health risk,' according to the Defense Nuclear Agency.

The Crossroads documents suggest otherwise. Eighty-four 'target' ships were placed close to the Baker explosion, with about a hundred others at a safe distance. Contamination of the target ships was severe and attempts to clean those still floating failed; most of them had to be sunk. Within six days, all the non-target ships had sailed into contaminated waters and become radioactive. Astonishingly, the US navy had succeeded in irradiating nearly 200 ships without any real idea of how to decontaminate them.

What happened next was to have a curious parallel six years later, after the first British test at Monte Bello. The report on Crossroads presented to the congressional hearings goes on: 'It was only after the radioactive ships reached San Francisco and other major ports, followed by extensive experimentation and work, that the levels of radioactivity were substantially reduced. In the meantime, the sailors received radiation doses as they lived and worked aboard.' The British, of course, were luckier than the Americans: they had only four radioactive ships to deal with, whereas the Americans had around a hundred left after the target ships had been sunk. (The US navy managed to irradiate so many ships that the Pacific Fleet was left short.)

Radiation protection officers complained of a 'hairy-chested' attitude to the dangers of radiation on the part of officers, who passed on their disdain of unseen hazards to their men. The official Decontamination Report on the whole of Operation Crossroads records that General Leslie Groves, the head of the Manhattan Project, 'is very much afraid of claims being instituted by men who participated in the Bikini tests'.

This example of what happens when secret documents are declassified, which I reported in the *Sunday Times* in May 1983, offered little cheer to the British government. Unfortunately, it had decided on its defence against the veterans' claims long before the horrible prospect of a full Royal Commission, complete with public hearings, raised its unwelcome visage. Before the Australians arrived in London, part of that defence was scientifically shaky. By the time they left, it was clear that the British tests had been conducted in a cavalier manner which far from justified ministers' confident assertions that everything had gone according to plan.

CHAPTER SIX

A case to answer

The response of the British government to any criticism of the bomb tests is remarkable for the degree of certainty with which it presents two questionable assertions. This confidence has been a consistent feature of all ministerial replies on the subject, whether they have come from Geoffrey Pattie, as Minister of State for Defence Procurement, his successor, Adam Butler, or from Margaret Thatcher herself. The only discernible difference since the first ministerial replies in January 1983 is the note of irritation which has crept in since Butler became spokesman.

Here is Geoffrey Pattie, writing to Liberal MP David Alton, in January 1983. The tone is confident but concerned. 'The safety arrangements made for our 1950s' test operations are still considered to have been very satisfactory. Everyone who was liable to a radiation exposure was issued with a personal dose monitoring device and the records of the measurements made by these dosimeters are available today, some twenty-five to thirty years later; this of itself is some proof of the attention we have continually paid to safety.

'The recorded doses conform to the radiological safety standards which were enforced at the time . . . Even by today's standards, radiation exposures to these levels are considered not to increase significantly the risk of an individual contracting cancer.'

Pattie goes on, in a tone of the utmost reasonableness, to deal with the government's survey. 'The Ministry of Defence continues to believe that no significant health damage was caused by the 1950s' test programme but, recognizing the concerns now being expressed, decided that it was necessary to carry out a survey to establish whether or not this assessment is valid. This survey, which we announced on 12 January 1983, will produce statistically valid data against which claims can be judged objectively.'

Radiation and its effects are notoriously difficult subjects for the lay person. Superficially, Pattie's letter sounds a pretty fair way of going about things. The government was confident nothing was wrong but accepted its responsibility to allay public concern. The government presumably hoped that, with little firm evidence to back up the anecdotal claims of veterans that parts of the test programme were a shambles, the subject would go away. They would also have been right in thinking that delving into radiological standards, which involves difficult arguments about the effects of radiation, not to mention a willingness to take on international regulatory organizations, was beyond the resources of many veterans and journalists.

This thwarted hope may lie behind the impatient tone adopted by Adam Butler nearly two years later in a letter to the MP of a Brighton veteran, Colin Avey. 'Contrary to Mr Avery's [*sic*] inference that something may have gone wrong, I am not aware of any excessive exposure to radiation in any part of the nuclear test programme,' the minister snapped.

This sentence is interesting for two reasons. First, there is the fact that Butler has not even bothered to get Avey's name right, a discourtesy which hints at his impatience with the subject. Second, Butler shows a remarkable ignorance of the issue on which it has fallen to him to be the government's spokesman. One presumes that Butler attempted at least to acquaint himself with major incidents that happened at the tests before arriving at his optimistic opinion on whether anyone was exposed to 'excessive' radiation.

So to take just one example: why was Butler not aware of the high levels of radiation to which RAF and RAAF crew were exposed after the Totem I blast at Emu Field? Contamination of the Australian planes was so severe that the Australian air force was furious about the hazard to which its men had been exposed. As for the British aircrew, an RAF officer, Wing Commander Dhenin, while on board the RAF Canberra which sampled the cloud, got nearly 50 per cent more than the highest level of gamma radiation exposure permitted for personnel at the tests.

Butler's surprising ignorance of a serious contamination hazard at the Totem I blast is symptomatic of the general unreliability of the government's assurances on the bomb tests. Its statements can be divided into two parts, each as unreliable as the other.

One is that safety arrangements were so satisfactory that no one could have been exposed to high levels of radiation. The other is that the low levels of radiation which most of the exposed men encountered are not hazardous. The rest of this chapter will demonstrate the untruth of the first assertion. The next chapter will set out reasons for disbelieving the second.

In September 1950, just two years before Britain's first atom bomb exploded in the Monte Bello Islands, Air Vice-Marshall E. D. Davis, of the Ministry of Supply, received a secret memo from the Health Physics Division at the Atomic Energy Research Establishment at Harwell. The writer, Group-Captain David Wilson, wrote to say just how unprepared the RAF was to take part in atomic tests.

'I realize that this is not in any way in my province or terms of reference, and, indeed, amounts to criticism of Service matters to an outside source [Ministry of Supply], but I feel that it is sufficiently important for me to risk this,' Wilson explained a little nervously. But he wanted to raise 'several purely domestic RAF problems' which had not been fully appreciated. 'These are enhanced by the general fact <u>that all radioactivity is potentially highly dangerous and extremely insidious.</u>' (Underlining as in original text.)

'There is *no* special clothing or equipment for troops engaged in handling sources' of radiation, Wilson said. Although plans to train personnel to take part in the tests were being prepared, the RAF had no instruments to measure levels of radioactivity. Nor did it have dosimeters to measure the exposure of individuals to radiation. 'There is *no* arrangement, as far as I know, for any form of air monitoring or for protection of aircraft, nor for their decontamination,' he went on.

This was in spite of the fact that 'a sample of metal similar to Sunderland [flying boat] hull contaminated here in August has remained badly contaminated for over six weeks,' the memo records. Wilson says that 'it has hitherto been regarded as mandatory that organizations dealing with radioactive materials must have an overall protection plan to counteract the effects of radiation.' The gist of his memo is that it would be a good idea if such a plan were drawn up.

It is perhaps the fault of the rushed nature of Britain's bomb testing programme that preparations were so behind at this stage. But a tendency to underestimate risk and place too much reliance on the efficiency of safety arrangements is a consistent theme of the weapons tests. Much greater detail is available on the Australian tests, simply because of the Australian Royal Commission, but there is little reason, judging by anecdotal evidence, to suppose the hydrogen bomb tests at Christmas Island were much better. If anything, the risk to servicemen at the hydrogen bomb trials was potentially greater, because of the massive yield of thermonuclear weapons.

The picture which has emerged of the Australian tests is remarkable for the extent to which things went wrong. From the testimony of those who were there, and from studying formerly secret documents, a terrifying catalogue of errors can be put together:

- Lord Penney has admitted that the Totem I blast at Emu Field in 1953 should not have been exploded. The bomb caused a black mist to pass over Wallatinna Station, an aboriginal settlement, where aborigines claim many of their number became sick and even died.

- Before the Royal Commission was set up, the British government admitted to only one incident in which aborigines strayed into a heavily-contaminated area. Not only is this claim nonsense – ex-servicemen have reported numerous incidents in which aborigines were spotted in prohibited areas – but even this single event was originally covered up because of its potential political impact on the future of the test programme. Servicemen were threatened with being imprisoned or shot if they talked about it.

• Members of both the British and Australian air forces were exposed to unacceptably high levels of radiation during an exercise to sample the radioactive cloud at the Totem I explosion. The risk extended to ground crew who handled the planes when they returned from the mission.

• Equipment used to monitor individuals' exposure to radiation was unreliable. Film badges gave different readings from pocket-sized personal dosimeters carried by the same person. Sometimes, film badges were not collected at all.

• Predictions of where atomic clouds would travel were often hopelessly wrong and they frequently passed across large chunks of Australia.

• Methods of measuring fallout on the mainland were hit or miss. Aerial surveys of ground contamination may have underestimated the amount of fallout by as much as ten times. At the first three explosions, long-range monitoring of the mainland was virtually non-existent.

• The series of minor trials conducted at Maralinga from 1955 to 1963 has left thousands of acres of land contaminated with radioactive plutonium and polonium, as well as highly toxic beryllium. Britain may be forced back to clean up this mess, an exercise which would involve removing tons of contaminated topsoil as well as the dangerous task of digging up twenty kilograms of plutonium buried in pits. One of the few installations in the world capable of dealing with this high-level radioactive waste is at Sellafield – that is, Windscale – in Cumbria.

There is now abundant evidence that, in some specific incidents, men were exposed to unacceptably high levels of radiation. It is also clear that methods of monitoring the exposure of individuals were not as reliable as the British government likes to suggest. Aborigines *were* exposed to radioactive hazards, both from airborne fallout and from contamination on the ground; they are still at risk from their trapping of rabbits which have burrowed among the plutonium pits at Maralinga. Radioactive clouds *did* drift over the mainland; because of faults in the monitoring systems, it is likely that they posed more of a hazard to the Australian population than has ever been admitted.

As if all this was not bad enough, it is now clear that the British did everything they could to deceive the Australians. The true size of the biggest bomb, the ninety-eight kiloton Mosaic II blast – nearly eight times as large as the Hiroshima bomb – was concealed from the Australian government for twenty-nine years. Penney has admitted suggesting that radioactive samples should be held back from Australian scientists for a few days to prevent them learning much about the nature of the bomb. A leading Australian scientist, Sir Mark Oliphant, was kept away from the tests on the grounds that the *Americans* considered him a security risk.

The Australians were far from blameless themselves. The safety committee set up to look after the health of the civilian population of Australia was as much worried about the effects of adverse publicity on the test programme as it was about the possibility of radioactive rain falling on the mainland. When it did express reservations about aspects of the tests, it seems to have done little to make the British amend their behaviour accordingly.

Much of the picture drawn above comes from formerly secret documents belonging to the British government. Some of the admissions come from Penney, the British scientist most closely associated with the test programme. It is curious, then, that British ministers – who had access to the documents while their contents were still concealed from the rest of us – have always been so confident about the safety of the tests.

Undoubtedly the most shocking admission to emerge about the tests came on the final day of the Royal Commission's London hearings, 18 March 1985. Penney accepted that, 'in hindsight', the Totem I test took place in unsafe conditions.

The two Totem tests, on 14 and 26 October 1953, were a rush job. They took place at Emu Field, in the South Australian desert, only 110 miles from the nearest inhabited area and within fifty miles of an aboriginal hunting area. They were held because of a decision that Britain should make 200 of the 600 atom bombs which the British Chiefs of Staff considered necessary for a joint British–American stockpile.

Britain did not have the capacity to produce sufficient pure plutonium for 200 bombs, so the Totem tests were designed to try out impure plutonium. 'The purpose of the test is simple,' says a contemporary memo to the Minister of Defence. 'It is to find out how much of the isotope 240 can be tolerated in plutonium used for military purposes . . . The need for carrying out this trial earlier is primarily due to the Chiefs of Staff proposal for doubling the production of fissile material.'

A Ministry of Supply document prepared five months before the test of the Totem I device predicts its yield as five kilotons, only a fifth of the size of the Hurricane bomb. It warns that fallout would be greatest if the weapon was exploded when the wind was blowing at the same speed and direction at all levels of the mushroom cloud. 'If these conditions should exist at the time of firing, then to avoid any risk of slight sickness this narrow wedge [of land] should not include a centre of population,' the report warns.

The first attempt to fire Totem I took place on 7 October. Standby was announced at eight in the morning, but by one o'clock the weather was so bad that it was called off. It rained heavily over the next few days and, frustratingly, standby could not be declared for a whole week. The weapon was fired at seven o'clock in the morning on 14 October: a circle of 200 yards radius around the steel tower on which the bomb was sitting was pulverized, indicating the bomb was much bigger than expected. In fact, it was ten kilotons, twice the size anticipated. Another official document released to the Royal Commission shows that the weapon was exploded in *precisely* the conditions – a steady wind at all levels of the cloud – which scientists had warned against five months before.

A narrow plume of radioactivity moved north-east from Emu,

passing over aborigines camped at Wallatinna Station and Welbourn Hill.

Ronald Siddons, one of the authors of the report which forecast how the Totem I bomb would behave, told the Royal Commission that the document underestimated the actual level of fallout by a factor of three. 'I believe that it was unduly risky to proceed with Totem I at the time it was fired,' he said.

Siddons, who is now a Deputy Director at AWRE at Aldermaston, said: 'If I had been asked at the time, my advice would have been not to fire it.'

As recently as 1983, the British Ministry of Defence denied any connection between Totem I and the black cloud which aborigines claimed to have seen over Wallatinna and Welbourn Hill after Totem I. But AWRE secretly asked meteorologists to look into the claim. One of them, Dr William Roach, confirmed to the Royal Commission that 'the fallout cloud would have been seen about mid-morning, possibly as an extended black curtain'.

It is not only the British government which has doubted the aborigines' claims. The Australian report, AIRAC 9, published in January 1983, says fallout from Totem I 'may have slightly exceeded' current recommendations on radiation dose limits for members of the public. It concludes that 'AIRAC has found no evidence that any Aboriginals were injured by the nuclear tests.'

The evidence presented to the Royal Commission leaves little doubt that the British were guilty of exploding an atom bomb in conditions that caused a thick cloud of fallout to pass over aboriginal encampments to the north-east. Two more pieces of evidence suggest the aborigines' claims of ill-health may be justified. The Royal Commission was told that, far from fallout at Wallatinna from Totem I being just over the present annual limit for members of the public, it could have been as much as 160 times that limit.

Dr Alice Stewart, the epidemiologist who has studied the Christmas Island tests, told the Commission that the number of aboriginal deaths from thyroid cancer and leukaemia in South Australia after the tests was too high. The South Australia Health Commission found that twenty-one aborigines living in the region of the atom bomb tests – Emu Field and Maralinga –

died of cancer between 1973 and 1980. This incidence of cancer deaths was higher than it should have been, according to Stewart.

The aborigines' claims of a black mist causing sickness and death in the desert in 1953 first came to light in 1980, when an aborigine called Yami Lester recalled an oily black cloud passing over his campsite at Wallatinna Station. He described how sickness and diarrhoea affected most of the aborigines camped there; he thought some of the very young and old might have died. Lester, who was about ten years old at the time, recalled how his eyes became sore and he lost the sight of first one, then the other.

Lester's claim was met with scorn by both the Australian and British authorities. Five years later, those official denials can be construed as adding insult to injury.

The British and Australian authorities have claimed to know of only one occasion when aborigines were found on a firing range. This incident took place at Maralinga on 14 May 1957, when a family of four was found to have spent the night camped at the bottom of the outer slope of the crater caused by the bomb code-named Marcoo. This bomb had been exploded the previous October as part of the Buffalo series of tests. Although it was a small weapon – only 1.5 kilotons – it was exploded on the ground and caused a good deal of contamination for its size.

The Australian AIRAC 9 report in 1983 says the dose received by the family 'cannot possibly have led to any identifiable ill effect'. Nevertheless, it clearly caused a panic at the time, according to evidence given to the Royal Commission. Geoff Eames, the barrister representing aborigines at the hearings in London, told Lord Penney that troops had been lined up and warned that they would be court-martialled if they spoke about the family to anyone outside the test site. They were told that the penalty they would get if found guilty was either death or thirty years in prison.

Rudi Marqueur, a captain in the Australian army at Maralinga, saw the male aborigine from the family walking from the contaminated area towards a caravan used for decontamination. Peter McClellan, the barrister assisting the Commission, asked

Marqueur whether the incident was 'of considerable concern' to those in charge of Maralinga. He replied: 'It certainly was, very much so, and at the same time we were warned ... everybody was warned to keep the whole situation quiet.'

Richard Durance, the Australian commander of the Maralinga range, was questioned about the incident by Geoff Eames during hearings in Australia. It became clear that the incident was so important that the Australian Minister of Supply, Howard Beale, was told about it. Here is the exchange:

EAMES ... that was a cause of acute political embarrassment, was it not?

DURANCE I think so.

EAMES And you were aware that political embarrassment was being felt very keenly by Minister Beale?

DURANCE Yes.

EAMES And you were aware that from the government's point of view, that incident must not leak out to the public?

DURANCE I was aware that he was pleased that it did not leak out.

For the family – a man, a woman, two children and their three dogs – the incident must have been terrifying. Suddenly plucked from their traditional lands by uniformed men, handed over to a security patrol, and moved many miles to the aboriginal reserve at Yalata: the events must have been the equivalent for Europeans of being scooped up by aliens from another planet. They were forced to take showers to get rid of contamination, a procedure that distressed them immensely. Rudi Marqueur was told, he said in evidence, that 'there was quite a lot of cahooing and screaming going on because the female did not want to have anyone else wash her under a shower, and her husband apparently also objected to the fact that she was going to go under that shower.' In fact, the family was lucky to arrive at Yalata still in possession of their dogs; the Minister of Supply, Beale, was furious when he heard that the dogs had not been shot.

In view of the stern warnings given to troops about revealing this incident, it is hardly surprising that many servicemen – like Gordon Wilson, the school caretaker from Hull, who regularly met aborigines in the prohibited area at Maralinga – just did not mention sightings to their superiors.

The AIRAC 9 report took an optimistic view of attempts to keep aborigines off the range: 'It is evident that strenuous attempts were made to prevent the entry of Aboriginals into hazardous areas, and although it would clearly be impossible to affirm that such an intrusion never took place, it seems most unlikely that any Aboriginals were present elsewhere than the fringes of the Prohibited Area at the firing times and in the period following them.'

The Royal Commission, on the other hand, heard a wealth of evidence that aborigines strayed into prohibited areas. Patrol officers charged with keeping them off the range at Maralinga complained that their task was hopeless in view of the huge area of land involved. Durance, the range commander, admitted he was not given specific instructions about keeping aborigines off the range when he took over in June 1956. He was questioned on the subject by Geoff Eames.

EAMES Were there any instructions in writing as to what steps should be taken to ensure that Aboriginal people did not move on to the range?
DURANCE If there were, I was not given them.

In fact, Durance seems to have taken over as commander in distinctly tense circumstances which involved some criticism of how the previous range commander, Colonel Dewar, had been running things. Eames asked Durance if he was given verbal instructions about the policy on the range to do with aborigines.

DURANCE The conversations were rather limited, as I was there to relieve Colonel Dewar and it was very embarrassing and we did not go into a great amount of detail. My function then was to try and find out what had not been done that had to be, and what had been done that should not have been done.

Durance went on to admit that, because a *possibility* that aborigines could have strayed on to the range had been demonstrated, the tests in 1956 and 1957 at Maralinga should have been cancelled. He told Geoff Eames that 'I cannot get away or deny the fact . . . that information that you have presented this morning . . . implying human beings there in 1956 and 1957 . . . the tests should not [have taken place].'

Before the commission was set up, a former RAF officer claimed he had found four dead aborigines in a crater after the tests at Maralinga. John Burke died of stomach cancer before he could give evidence at the hearings, but he said he also saw about 200 dead cockatoos and rabbits near the crater. Bill Grigsby, who was in the Royal Navy, told his wife before his own death in 1977 that he found aborigines camped in a bomb crater at Maralinga in 1962. Although the major weapons tests were over, minor trials were still going on. Grigsby said all the people in the small group in the crater were covered in sores. Patrick Connolly, who served in the RAF at Maralinga between 1959 and 1962, said he had seen large numbers of aborigines all over the restricted area.

During Lord Penney's evidence to the Royal Commission, Eames told him that one man had been responsible for clearing an area stretching a hundred miles from the range, and that the man concerned thought his job hopeless and just a public relations exercise. Penney said he had not known any of this; he believed the tests were taking place in an uninhabited wasteland.

The Totem I blast which put at risk aborigines at Wallatinna and Welbourn Hill also proved an unexpected radiation hazard for members of the British, Australian and American air forces. Their job was to fly through the radioactive cloud after the blast to take samples. The crew of the single British plane, an RAF Canberra, got high doses of radiation in spite of flying in a plane completely sealed with tape. The six Australian Lincolns, whose crews took no precautions against radiation, on British advice, picked up so much contamination there were fears for the safety of air and ground crews. The American crew of the two USAF

B-29s said the radioactivity from the cloud was the most intense they had ever encountered.

The Australian document, AIRAC 9, took a characteristically cheerful view of the contamination problem caused by Totem I. It said that 'radioactive contamination of the Lincoln aircraft flying from Woomera to track the cloud of the first Totem test was found to be heavier than anticipated' but concluded that it was 'most unlikely' that it had caused any injury to the crews.

The story which has unfolded since the publication of AIRAC 9 is much more worrying. Although the British Canberra which sampled the cloud only six minutes after the explosion had been sealed before take-off, the plane encountered so much radiation that Penney refused to allow it to carry out the same operation at the Totem II test twelve days later.

The Australians fared even worse. Squadron Leader Ray Turner, of the RAAF, told the Royal Commission that his plane flew into a cloud of red dust and could not get out of it. The meter for measuring external radiation – the only piece of monitoring equipment on board the plane – went to its maximum reading on entering the cloud and stayed there throughout the flight. Turner and the rest of the crew ate their rations on the plane and, unlike the Canberra crew who used oxygen, breathed contaminated air.

When the plane landed at Woomera, it was met by scientists who started running Geiger counters over everything. Turner said they went off like machine guns – 'They were making a hell of a noise, rather loud and rather fast.' His flying suit was taken away and he was told to take several showers.

One of the Australian planes landed at Williamtown air base, in New South Wales, after the sampling mission. The next day, an American airman walked round the Lincoln carrying a Geiger counter; all he could say was, 'Oh, shit . . . oh, shit.' The American had intended to take a lift on the plane back to its base at Richmond, near Sydney. But he told the crew he had decided to take the train instead. 'That bloody machine is hot,' he said. 'I'm not going anywhere near it.'

It was from the Americans, in fact, that the Australian air

force learned just how badly contaminated its planes were. An Australian report on the Totem tests released to the Royal Commission shows how unprepared the Australians were to deal with any hazard – unsurprisingly, since the British had told them there wasn't one.

'It was fortunate that the US Air Force element contained personnel very experienced in [decontamination] operations and were thus able to assist the operations commander at Richmond by advising him on the degree of contamination on aircraft and personnel and the safety precautions to be observed,' it says.

'It was only through seeking assistance of the US Air Force specialists and equipment that it was at all possible to ascertain that Lincoln aircraft and personnel had obtained any degree of contamination.

'The precaution to have the Lincoln aircraft which landed at Williamtown inspected proved the importance of this aspect and how ignorance on the part of RAAF personnel on matters of this nature could possibly have proved dangerous.'

Squadron Leader Turner told the Royal Commission that ground staff refused to work on his Lincoln the day after it had landed and been found to be radioactive. Some ground staff *did* work on the contaminated Lincolns before it was realized how radioactive they were: one man spent three hours on the wing of the hottest of the Lincolns on the day after the cloud sampling operation.

The Australian air force was furious about the incident. A senior officer wrote angrily: 'We were firmly told this was not a hazard . . . It does appear there was a hazard . . . It would seem that this service is not informed of the hazard its own personnel may undergo.'

The Americans, by contrast, knew exactly what they were doing. The British had allowed them to send two B-29s to the test because the British embassy in Washington had made it clear to the UK government that the USAF intended to sample the Totem cloud whether the British gave permission or not.

In fact, an American air force plane had been allowed to take samples at Operation Hurricane. But by the time of the Totem tests, the US had failed to comply with a British request to hand over some of these samples – they were treating the British just as the British were treating the Australians. In the event, the Americans did hand over some of their samples after Totem I, but they sent the bulk to Guam for analysis. The samples were so radioactive that Guam could not handle them, and they were flown to Washington.

Although the risks to air and ground crew were most serious at Totem I, there is no doubt that incidents of planes becoming very radioactive happened at later tests. An RAF plane became 'substantially contaminated' during the Mosiac series of tests at Monte Bello in 1956, according to AIRAC 9. The hazard continued to exist during the Christmas Island tests: Christopher Donne, an RAF pilot who flew sampling missions at the hydrogen bomb tests, told the Royal Commission that 'on the last and largest of them I was subjected to high radiation levels and prevented from doing any more sampling work'. The British and Australian air and ground crews involved in sampling missions probably received some of the highest doses of any servicemen at the tests.

The British government's claim that it knows what doses individuals received rests on the premise that the system for monitoring personnel was both well administered and accurate. The evidence is that it was nowhere near as good as it is claimed to be.

A prerequisite of a really comprehensive monitoring system is that the procedure laid down is followed in every case. Brian Last, a fitter in the Australian air force, was issued with two film badges during his service at Maralinga in 1956. When he left, he took the second one with him. 'My daughter still has it today,' he told the Royal Commission. Last is not the only veteran who left the tests without handing in his film badge for checking. He also gave evidence that other people at Maralinga took their film badges apart out of curiosity – thus exposing the film and destroying the reading – and then put them back together again.

Doug Rickard, an Australian whose job was to issue small, pocket-size dosimeters to men who were going into areas where they might be at risk at Maralinga, has admitted making up the readings he was supposed to record when the dosimeters were returned. This was because each one had to be charged by battery before being handed out – many of the batteries were flat, he says, so the dosimeters didn't work. He would ask an individual where he had spent the day, and make up a dose accordingly.

Even when dosimeters and film badges *did* work, and *were* collected in for checking, the readings they gave were not always reliable. One of the many British documents released to the Royal Commission was an AWRE report which examined the reliability of film badges and small dosimeters.

It recorded an experiment during the Operation Buffalo trials at Maralinga in 1956. A mahogany model of a man was placed in a contaminated area, wearing both film badges and dosimeters. The report concluded that the film badge tended to *under-record* the dose received by the lower half of the body – including the genital organs – by 40 per cent. It also noted it was quite common for film badges and dosimeters worn simultaneously by the same person to show different readings.

When this evidence was raised with Penney, his response suggested that much of the measuring done at the tests was carried out with primitive equipment. In 1957, he said, there was 'a tremendous upheaval in health physics', the branch of science concerned with people's exposure to radiation. The reason was the catastrophic fire in a plutonium-producing pile at the Windscale bomb factory, which sent a plume of radiation south-east across the UK.

Penney was appointed to run the inquiry into the incident. 'What it taught me was that the instrumentation of the pile needed improving,' he told the Royal Commission. 'That although we thought we had got a lot of instruments, we weren't sure they were all running correctly.'

In other words, the instruments used for monitoring general levels of radioactivity in nuclear establishments and at the bomb tests were liable to error, on top of the doubts about the accuracy of equipment used to check the exposure of individuals. The knowledge came too late to improve matters at the bomb tests in Australia: the Windscale fire started the day *after* the last British atom bomb test took place on Australian territory.

Much time and effort went into working out the safest time to explode each weapon, the idea being to carry out the test at a time when the wind would carry the atomic cloud well away from populated areas, or at such a height that it would pose no threat. A lot of this effort seems to have been wasted; in fact, it looks suspiciously like a public relations exercise.

Thomas Brindley, an Australian soldier responsible for monitoring fallout at Maralinga, told the Royal Commission about a curious experience he had. After the very first test at the site, a blast code-named One Tree, Brindley was out to the east of the range. 'We heard on the radio . . . [that the] Minister for Supply had said that the fallout had gone harmlessly away to the northwest. And we were sitting below Coober Pedy in the fallout area, which is directly east.' Australians would obviously be much happier if fallout was drifting north-west across the desert towards mountainous Western Australia, instead of heading east towards populated New South Wales.

We have already seen how part of the fallout from Operation Hurricane drifted across the mainland at 10,000 feet instead of the much more innocuous 25,000 feet predicted. During the Royal Commission's hearings in London, Peter McClellan, the barrister assisting the commission, read out comparisons between the cloud paths predicted for various tests and where they actually went.

The cloud from the third test in the Buffalo series at Maralinga, for instance, was supposed to go just north of Brisbane, on the east coast of Australia. Where it actually went was just north of Sydney, about 400 miles further south. When it came to the fourth Buffalo test, fallout was intended to go north of Brisbane again. What actually happened became clear in this exchange between McClellan and Penney:

MCCLELLAN The observed pattern –
PENNEY (*interrupting*) Goes everywhere!
MCCLELLAN Half to three-quarters of Australia. At the time,

did it become known that the cloud had behaved so differently . . . was any concern expressed?

PENNEY When that was known, to my knowledge, no concern
was expressed.

The cloud from the biggest British bomb tested in Australia,
the 98-kiloton blast known as Mosaic II, was supposed to drift
harmlessly out to sea from the Monte Bello Islands. Instead, the
wind changed and blew fallout across the small towns on the
coast of nearby Western Australia – Onslow, Roebourne, Dam-
pier and Port Hedland. This event was the cause of the frantic
signal to the British from the Australian government which demanded to know what was going on.

Other clouds – Operation Hurricane and the second Totem
test – simply got lost. The overall picture, in which radioactive
clouds can be seen drifting unpredictably across populated areas
of Australia, is hard to reconcile with claims that the Australian
population was never put at risk.

The extent to which the population of Australia was exposed to
radiation from the tests is difficult to assess because of the inad-
equacy of the efforts made to measure it. No information at all is
available on long-range fallout from the first three tests – Operations Hurricane and Totem – because no aerial surveys were
made to look for it.

At the later tests, aerial surveys were carried out to check for
fallout at considerable distances from the tests; from Totem
onwards, monitoring stations were set up on the ground to collect fallout. Evidence given to the Royal Commission cast doubt
on the effectiveness of all these systems in giving accurate
measurements. But the spirit in which the monitoring was done
is clear, and explains the confidence with which rather inad-
equate data was used as the basis of assurances to the Australian
people about the safety of the tests.

The purpose of setting up the monitoring systems was revealed quite clearly during exchanges between Peter McClellan
and Lord Penney during the Commission's London hearings.
McClellan said the monitoring stations were set up specifically

to check fallout from the tests. 'Was that done', he asked, 'because of concern [that] there may be some safety problems?'

'No,' said Penney, dismissing the notion that there could be any danger to the Australian people. 'It was done *to confirm it was all right*.' (My italics.) When McClellan pressed him, Penney expanded on the theme in a way which stressed the public relations nature of the exercise. 'It was to demonstrate it was safe,' he insisted, adding, 'We were sure, but there's nothing like being doubly sure.'

It seems a curious departure-point for a scientific investigation. It may also explain why the exercise was carried out with rather unreliable equipment. Ground monitoring was done by festooning the countryside with sticky paper, which was supposed to catch particles of fallout. McClellan suggested to Penney that the sticky-paper method hadn't worked very well at all. 'Well,' said Penney, 'I can't really say yes or no. They don't look as if they'd be too good but they did give a reading.'

The problem with the sticky-paper method was that it was adversely affected by rain. Unfortunately, the other system used for monitoring on the ground, air pumps which measured airborne contamination passing through them, was also unreliable. McClellan raised these problems with Donald Stevens, an Australian scientist who was director of the Australian Radiation Laboratory from 1956 to 1977 and a member from 1956 of the Australian committee set up to look after the safety of the civilian population during the British bomb tests.

MCCLELLAN You were also involved in the monitoring of fallout in Australia outside the declared area [the official danger zone]. In this programme, two types of equipment were used, air pumps and sticky-paper samplers. You recall the air pumps ran into some problems, however, particularly in outback Australia – for example, dust clogged some filter papers and inhibited the standard flow of air through them, with the result that in some areas there may have been an underestimate of airborne contamination at ground level. Are you able to give me any idea of the order of underestimate that would have been involved?

STEVENS No, I could not.

MCCLELLAN Could it be in the order of hundreds or thousands of per cent? What sort of range would you expect?

STEVENS No, I would be completely guessing, Your Honour.

McClellan then asked what happened to the sticky-paper samplers when it rained. 'Well, the sticky paper was a gum form on a plastic base, as it were,' said Stevens, 'and under heavy rain conditions this became ... lost its tackiness ... lost its ability to hold the deposit on it.'

MCCLELLAN Well, have we reached the position then, sir, [that] by 1958 it was recognized by the Atomic Weapons Tests Safety Committee [the Australian safety committee] that there were problems in the collection of fallout information from both the air-pump method and the sticky-paper method?

STEVENS There were some uncertainties, yes.

The other method of checking fallout on the mainland was through aerial surveys made by planes flying at 500 feet. At the Royal Commission hearings, it emerged that the actual readings made by this method have to be multiplied by ten to give a genuine reflection of the level of contamination on the ground. But the Atomic Weapons Tests Safety Committee used the actual readings to give assurances to the public about the levels of fallout from the tests.

All in all, the systems used for monitoring the mainland are curiously flawed as a basis for the soothing noises made about the lack of danger from fallout from the tests. But, as Penney has revealed, their purpose was less to find out what was going on than to reinforce a preconceived notion that there was no risk to the public.

As well as the twelve atom bomb tests which took place in Australia, Britain also carried out a series of related experiments at Emu Field and Maralinga. The experiments started at Emu in 1953, moved to Maralinga in 1955 and did not end until 1963, long after the last atom bomb test.

They were shrouded in even greater secrecy than the actual bomb tests, and with good reason from the British government's point of view. They have left large quantities of plutonium at Maralinga to this day, a serious problem since aborigines want to move back into the area. They were also politically sensitive by the end of the 1950s; Britain agreed to a moratorium on weapons testing at the end of 1958 and the minor trials could be interpreted as a breach of the spirit, if not the letter, of the agreement.

Hundreds of experiments were carried out: the exact number is not known, since accurate records have not been kept. Little bits of information have been pieced together, but we still do not have a complete picture of what went on.

Under the innocuous title of 'Vixens', a series of experiments took place to determine what would happen to an atom bomb if it was involved in an accident – a plane crash, for example. ('We always had words that had nothing to do with the subject,' Penney explained cheerfully to the Royal Commission.) Bombs were exposed to intense fires to see if they could withstand great heat without actually going off.

Another series of minor trials – 'Tims' – was intended to test the compressibility of plutonium. The idea was to observe the effect on plutonium of a shock wave caused by high explosives. Would that have involved dispersion of plutonium, Penney was asked during his evidence to the Royal Commission. 'Yes,' he replied. 'Into the atmosphere?' 'Yes.'

Other experiments were designed to try out devices for starting an atomic explosion. We can get some idea of how many experiments took place overall by looking at periods for which we know the dates of the experiments. In 1953, a number of 'Kittens' experiments took place at the same time as the two Totem bombs were tested at Emu Field. Five experiments were carried out between 26 September and 17 October. In 1955, 'Kittens' trials were held regularly at Maralinga from April to June. In July, they were followed by a series of 'Tims' experiments.

In 1959, when the major trials were over and during the voluntary moratorium on nuclear testing, dozens of experiments took place between March and August at Maralinga. There were four separate series of trials – 'Rats', 'Kittens', 'Tims' and 'Vixens'. In December that year, the Australians were asked to consider a further series of experiments in 1960. The British made clear they were anxious to avoid publicity, because of international discussions on a permanent test ban treaty. The Australians were as accommodating as ever: the 1960 series of experiments included twelve 'Vixens' trials, which involved detonations and burnings. The experiments ended in 1963; in September that year, the Atomic Weapons Tests Safety Committee prepared a paper which noted extensive plutonium contamination at Maralinga.

In 1967, when a decision was taken to close the Maralinga range, a team of Royal Engineers and AWRE staff went to Australia to clean up the mess. The exercise, known as Operation Brumby, is described in a secret report by a scientist called Noah Pearce which was leaked to the *National Times* of Australia in 1984.

The Pearce report shows that tractors were used to churn plutonium into the topsoil over an area of 500 acres at Maralinga. When this had been done, some areas were still so contaminated that they had to be covered with clean topsoil. Since the area is known for its dust storms, it is likely that breaking up the plutonium in this way simply enhanced its chances of being blown across an even wider area.

In 1972, AIRAC 9 reported, there had been 'heavy loss' of topsoil at Taranaki, the section of the Maralinga site which had been most heavily contaminated by the minor trials. As well as the plutonium churned into the topsoil, there are nineteen pits at Maralinga which contain 20 kilograms of plutonium mixed in with other material. Plutonium is so dangerous that less than a third of a milligram will give you a 50 per cent chance of getting cancer if it lodges in your lung.

Seventy acres of land have been fenced off at Maralinga, but there is plutonium contamination well outside this area. The scale of the problem posed by the state of Maralinga became clear at hearings of the Royal Commission in Australia in October 1984. Peter McClellan asked Dr Keith Lokan, director of the Australian Radiation Laboratory, how long the area would have to be kept under surveillance if it was allowed to remain in its present state. Lokan's answer was uncompromising: one million years. The prospect clearly alarmed McClellan.

MCCLELLAN A million years. You keep the Commonwealth
    police on overtime, six-weekly vacational tours, and you
    continue to fence. That is what no change means, is that
    right?

Lokan agreed that it was. McClellan asked him whether the experiments using plutonium should have been carried out at Maralinga. He replied: 'My view is that they should not have been conducted, because plutonium has a very long half life [the time required for half the substance to lose its radioactivity] and the problem is with us then for a very long time.'

If Australia decides to remove all the contamination that remains at Maralinga, someone will have to carry out a massive and unpleasant job: the removal of hundreds of acres of topsoil contaminated with plutonium, and the excavation of nineteen pits containing large amounts of plutonium. There is also the question of how to dispose of the resulting quantity of high-level radioactive waste. Peter McClellan made his thinking clear during his questioning of Dr Lokan. 'Let me ask what some might consider to be the more relevant question,' he suggested, after a discussion of possible sites for the waste in Australia. 'Do you know whether or not there is such a site in Great Britain for the disposition of such waste?' The drift of his question was such that he did not need to mention Windscale by name.

Because they had so little say in the early tests, the Australians decided to set up their own committee to protect the civilian population during the later tests. It came into being in 1955, as the Maralinga Safety Committee, and turned itself into the Atomic Weapons Tests Safety Committee the following year. It was chaired first by Professor Sir Leslie Martin, then by Penney's former colleague from Los Alamos, Professor Sir Ernest Titterton.

The committee was, to say the least, ineffective; if the British had taken its advice seriously, the tests would probably have ground to an early halt. It was not only ignored but also seems to have failed, on one occasion, to convey to Penney a vital piece of information about the safety of the aboriginal population. In addition the committee seems to have identified with British interests to the point where it worried about the possibility of radioactive rain less because of its possible effect on the mainland than because it might engender publicity harmful to the tests.

On 9 May 1956, the committee held its seventh meeting. Three bomb tests had taken place so far, at Operations Hurricane and Totem. The Mosaic series was well under way in the Monte Bello Islands: the first of the two bombs in the exercise would be tested a week later. The British were now drawing up plans for their first tests at Maralinga – the Buffalo series, which would start in September that year.

The committee was worried about fallout from the tests due to be held at Maralinga. The chances of getting winds blowing into the area of land considered safest for the test were 'slight'. The committee had sought technical information from Britain on the types of weapons to be tested; because of the amount of fallout the bombs were likely to produce, 'the tests might have to be restricted to relatively small atomic devices'.

These restrictions – limiting the Maralinga tests to small bombs and only firing the weapons on the rare occasions when the wind was in the right direction – would have made it difficult for the British to go ahead with the tests planned for Maralinga. McClellan asked Donald Stevens, who joined the committee just after this meeting, exactly what the restrictions implied in the memo would have meant.

His reply suggested that the bombs should be no bigger than ten kilotons, and should be exploded in the air or at least on top of high towers to minimize fallout. 'That memorandum presents a very bleak picture for the future of British nuclear tests in Australia, does it not?' commented McClellan.

The British, however, either never heard of the committee's reservations, or ignored them. The first test at Maralinga, the One Tree blast in September, was fifteen kilotons. The final test at Maralinga, the Taranaki test in October 1957, was twenty-five kilotons. And the Marcoo test in October 1956, although it was a small 1.5-kiloton bomb, was actually exploded on the ground – the type of blast which causes the most fallout.

At its sixth meeting, a month before, the committee also received advice which should have prevented the use of Maralinga as a test site at all. The advice, on the risk to aborigines, was never passed on to Penney. When the British were looking for mainland sites to test bombs, Penney had decided any place chosen had to be a hundred miles from inhabited areas. He did this by looking at the distance of Las Vegas from the Nevada site in the US – seventy miles – and adding a bit on for the sake of caution.

But at its sixth meeting, in April 1956, the committee heard a reply from AWRE at Aldermaston to its request for information on the risk from radiation to aborigines living in their tribal state – nearly naked and with bare feet. It said that, because they did not have even the small protection afforded by clothes and shoes, aborigines could be exposed to *five times less* radiation than people in European dress. Translated into distances, the advice meant that 'for a nominal [20 kilotons] burst, the acceptable level would occur at a distance of about 240 miles' from the site of the test.

There were thirteen aboriginal settlements within 200 miles of Maralinga, several of them just beyond the hundred-mile limit laid down by Penney. The advice given to the committee made Maralinga a most unsuitable place for the tests: Penney told the Royal Commission he was completely unaware of it. Needless to say, the tests went ahead.

The committee did, however, warn the Australian cabinet about radioactive rain – but not because it thought it was a hazard. On 13 August 1956, it made a top-secret report to the cabinet, pointing out that after the second Monte Bello test, 'some very low activity was observed in rainwater samples at great distances from the site'. The levels were absolutely harmless, the committee adds, but 'the results were given publicity and magnified by the press into what became practically a political crisis.'

Instead of looking into ways of preventing radioactive rain, the committee simply warned the Australian government that 'we appreciate the political difficulties that radioactive rain might stimulate and we have to point out that it is always a possibility'.

The committee goes on in the same report to ask for advice on what it should do if a situation arose in which 'dangerous' levels of fallout got into drinking water. This could happen at Oodnadatta, more than 250 miles from Maralinga, if rain washed fallout from a roof into a nearly empty tank containing drinking water.

'Such accidents could occur,' the report says, 'and the Safety Committee would have to take necessary action, such as has been necessary in the US Nevada tests from time to time. It might also become necessary to evacuate a homestead for a few hours while fallout decayed.' The committee wanted to know 'the action it should take' if such an unlikely event happened. It is easy to see why the committee was worried. If low levels of radioactivity in rainwater had provoked 'practically a political crisis' two months before, the evacuation of a homestead, if it leaked out, might put a stop to the tests once and for all.

On 12 March 1984, Geoffrey Pattie, Minister of State for Defence Procurement, stated the British government's position on the tests during a debate initiated by the Liberal MP, David Alton.

'I would be the first to agree that it would be entirely wrong to deny compensation if harm were proved,' he said. 'But it is equally wrong to believe that the natural sympathy that one has for those who are suffering from serious illness, or who have been bereaved, is in itself a justification for denying *the available scientific and other evidence*. Our claim that the tragic illnesses suffered by some of those who took part in the tests were not caused by exposure to radiation from those tests *is based on that scientific evidence* and does not reflect a lack of sympathy for those afflicted.' (My italics.) This seems a strange statement for anyone in full possession of the facts to make.

CHAPTER SEVEN

'Keep them confused'

President Eisenhower on what to tell the public
about the hydrogen bomb, 1953

President Eisenhower's attitude to telling the public about America's hydrogen bomb programme was simple. 'Keep them [the people] confused,' he told the chairman of the Atomic Energy Commission, the body set up by the US government to control nuclear energy, in 1953. The same approach has been applied, whether for purposes of deliberate obfuscation or because members of the public are considered too stupid to understand it, to the issue of the dangers posed by exposure to radiation.

The simplest way to look at the effects of radiation is to divide them into two categories: those effects which are related to the size of the dose, and those which are not. In the first category comes radiation sickness, the illness which was graphically demonstrated to the world after the bombing of Hiroshima and Nagasaki. The victim suffers from a whole range of symptoms, including diarrhoea, sickness and exhaustion; if the dose received is very high, the victim will probably die within two months. The smaller the dose, the more likely it becomes that the person will survive. Below a certain dose, the victim will not suffer radiation sickness at all.

This means there is a threshold, a dose below which radiation sickness will not be caused. Other examples of this type of effect are hair loss and skin burns. If you are exposed to a low enough dose of radiation, you simply will not suffer from them.

The effects which fall into the second category, the induction of cancer and genetic effects, do not work in this way at all. There is no dose of radiation so small that it cannot produce cancer or a change that will appear in a future generation. Unlike radiation sickness, the severity of the effect is not

143

affected by the dose. You either get cancer or a genetic effect or you do not. If the dose gets bigger, it is *your chance of suffering the effect* that increases. Put simply, this means that the higher the dose, the more people in the exposed group will develop cancer or a genetic defect because of it.

This hypothesis is now accepted by members of the scientific community, from Dr Alice Stewart, of Birmingham University, a stern opponent of nuclear power, to Sir Edward Pochin, consultant to the director of the National Radiological Protection Board, who takes a much more optimistic view than Stewart of the effects of low-level radiation. But it took a long time for the lack of a threshold to be accepted; in the early days of radiation protection, the assumption of the scientific community was that a threshold did exist.

The conduct of the debate in the 1950s is a good example of how difficult it is for members of the public to obtain unbiased information about the subject of radiation. Pro-nuclear scientists argued confidently and noisily in favour of the threshold hypothesis, as if it were established fact rather than the subject of violent controversy. The public could certainly be forgiven if it was confused.

The idea that there was no threshold for genetic effects was articulated by a highly respectable scientific body as early as 1947. A committee set up in Britain by the Medical Research Council (MRC) reported in February that year that there did not seem to be any dose too low to produce a genetic effect. 'All quantitative experiments show that even the smallest doses of radiation produce a genetic effect,' it reported, 'there being no threshold dose below which no genetic effect is induced.'

But the debate did not move from the laboratory into the public domain until the early 1950s. The cause was the atmospheric bomb tests. For the first time, the public was being exposed to radiation in addition to that from the natural background – which comes from sources like the sun – through worldwide fallout from the explosions.

Very sensibly, people in Britain and the US became worried about fallout; their concern was unwelcome to their governments, who were busily letting off bombs and did not want to

stop. The tenor of the argument about whether a threshold existed was heavily influenced by this consideration; the claim that
no harm was being done rested on the notion that the amounts of
radiation to which the public was being exposed were too small
to do any harm.

The debate was hardly conducted in a spirit of free and frank
scientific exchange. In 1955, two scientists from Colorado University, Ray Lanier and Theodore Puck, challenged an assertion
by the American Atomic Energy Commission that the tests
posed an insignificant hazard. The Governor of Colorado,
Edwin C. Johnson, responded by saying Lanier and Puck
'should be arrested'.

In 1956, the prestigious US National Academy of Sciences set
up committees to examine the hazards of radiation. One committee came to the same conclusion as the MRC in Britain, that
there was no threshold for genetic effects. Curiously, another of
the committees concluded there *was* a safe limit for one particularly dangerous radioactive substance, strontium 90.

The controversy continued in 1957. An article in *Science*
magazine suggested for the first time that there was no threshold
for leukaemia. The article, by E. B. Lewis, of the California Institute of Technology, came under attack in the US but received
support from Andrei Sakharov in Russia.

At the same time, American citizens who wrote to President
Eisenhower with their worries about fallout from the bomb tests
were being sent a reassuring statement written by Dr Charles L.
Dunham, director of a division of the US Atomic Energy Commission. 'Most of the leading pathologists believe that a
threshold dose of radiation exists below which exposure to radiation will not cause leukaemia,' Dunham said.

Another scientist, Dr Austin M. Brues, director of a research
division at the Argonne National Laboratory, which is run by
the US Department of Energy, was also arguing in favour of a
threshold. 'There are also good reasons from what we know
about the nature of cancer to suspect that the hazard goes down
faster than the initiating agent,' Brues said.

In an article in *Life* magazine in February 1958 entitled 'The
Compelling Need for Nuclear Tests', two more US-based

scientists, Dr Edward Teller and Dr Albert Latter, gave their view that radiation in small doses might not be harmful and might even be helpful.

Teller, a Hungarian scientist who went to the US before the Second World War, was known as the father of the American hydrogen bomb. He was also one of Linus Pauling's chief opponents in the argument about nuclear testing. Pauling was infuriated by all these statements from scientists which mini-mized the risk from fallout and suggested there was a threshold below which no harm would be done.

'There is no safe dose of radiation or of radioactive material,' he warned in 1958. 'Even small amounts do harm.' Pauling's view was quickly vindicated. From 1958 onwards, the body which sets international standards for radiation exposure – the International Commission on Radiological Protection – aban-doned the threshold hypothesis when it was working out its recommendations on exposure.

It was far from being the end of the matter, however. The debate about the effects of radiation simply shifted ground. Once the notion of a threshold had been abandoned, it was no longer possible to set limits which would give people *absolute protection* from damage caused by radiation. The limits are actually levels at which the risk – of getting cancer or undergoing some kind of change which will appear in a later generation – is considered so small as to be acceptable. To do this, you need a pretty good idea of how many cancers are likely to be induced by a certain dose of radiation. That is a question to which scientists still cannot agree an answer.

That a controversy exists over the effects of low-level radiation is something you would never begin to suspect if you confined your reading to official British statements about the bomb tests. Government ministers have simply ignored the issue by refer-ring to international standards set for exposure to radiation in industry today.

'Safety precautions were taken that compare favourably with the international standards in force today,' the junior Defence Minister, Geoffrey Pattie, told MPs in March 1984. 'These limits were comparable with those which apply to radiation workers today,' the Prime Minister, Margaret Thatcher, said in January 1985.

Of course, the degree of trust that can be placed in those limits depends on the standing of the organization that recommended them. In this case, the body which makes the recommendations is the International Commission on Radiological Protection (ICRP). It is an organization with close links to the nuclear industry, with a poor record when it comes to speaking out on man-made radiation hazards, and which has itself admitted that its limits are set at a level which does not hinder the commercial development of nuclear power.

Scientists interested in radiation held their first congresses in the 1920s. In 1928, they set up an organization which was the forerunner of the ICRP, the International Commission of X-ray and Radium Protection. Its last meeting before the Second World War took place in 1938; it did not meet again until 1950, when it held a congress in London and turned itself into the ICRP. From time to time, after reviewing the available evidence, it issues recommendations on the radiation doses permitted for workers in the nuclear industry and for members of the public. In one form or another, these limits, which themselves have no legal status, are incorporated into law by many countries throughout the world, including Britain.

The commission has thirteen members who sit for periods of four years. New members are elected by existing members. The ICRP also has four expert committees to advise it on subjects like the effects of radiation. Members of the commission and its committees are supposed to be chosen for their expert knowledge of radiation protection; in fact, it is almost unheard-of for any outspoken critics of the nuclear industry to get on to the commission. It is dominated by scientists who have links with either the commercial exploitation of nuclear energy or governmental organizations concerned with the development of nuclear energy.

Dr Rosalie Bertell, an expert on cancer and probably its most implacable critic, says that the ICRP's structure has ensured that 'participation in standard-setting has been dominated by colleagues from the military, the civilian nuclear establishment and the medical radiological societies, who nominate one another'. These people, she says, have 'a vested interest in the use of radiation and depreciation of the risks in its use'.

A more surprising critic is the American physicist, Professor Karl Z. Morgan, until 1973 a member of the commission and chair of one of its expert committees. Morgan expressed his doubts about it when he spoke to a conference at Guy's Hospital in London in 1979. The ICRP 'has never been willing to offend the establishment and I'm not sure it's an organization I would trust with my life,' he said.

In January 1985, a British academic called Patrick Green published an MSc thesis on the low-level radiation controversy in which he analysed membership of the ICRP from 1959 to 1981. In that period, a total of ninety-one scientists could have served on the commission if each member had retired after one four-year period. Only thirty-seven had, demonstrating the self-perpetuating nature of the body.

Green found that the dominant influence on the ICRP in this period came from scientists connected with the nuclear industry. Two men each had a total of twenty-six years' service on the commission and its committees; they were John Dunster, a British physicist who also held senior positions with the United Kingdom Atomic Energy Authority, and Henri Jammet, a French physicist who headed a department at the French atomic energy commission.

After these two, there were three scientists who had served for twenty-three years each; all had connections with governmental nuclear establishments. One held an important position with the Argentine atomic energy commission, for instance.

In the period Green looked at, fourteen of the thirty-seven scientists who sat on the commission were physicists, always the most hawkish people in the scientific community on the subject of nuclear energy. 'The biological and environmental sciences have been poorly represented,' Green commented.

His conclusion on the ICRP is damning. Far from being concerned with examining the fundamental principles of radiation protection, he says, it 'has shown itself to be an organization concerned with the commercial exploitation of nuclear energy'. The ICRP's own publications suggest as much. When it issued recommended levels of exposure in 1966, it accompanied them with this revealing statement: 'The commission believes that this level provides reasonable latitude for the expansion of atomic energy programs in the foreseeable future.' It even went on to admit that the limit it suggested might not have got the risk right.

The commission was in a unique position when it reformed itself in the 1950s to act as the public's watchdog on fallout from the atmospheric tests: it did not. So it is hardly surprising that British ministers feel quite safe hiding behind the ICRP's skirts when it comes to defending their record on the bomb tests.

The radiation limits set for the British tests are, to some extent, a red herring. What matters is the kind of dose people received, not the amount to which they could, in theory, have been exposed. The prescribed limits do, however, give us a glimpse of just how dismissive British scientists were of the risks of radiation.

Any discussion of doses of radiation is bedevilled by the multiplicity of units used to measure it. Substantial changes in terminology have taken place since the 1950s. The standard unit now in use to measure the impact of radiation on the body is the sievert, which is in turn divided into millisieverts, each representing a thousandth of a sievert. The sievert is simply a unit which takes into account the effect of different types of radiation on human beings: for the sake of simplicity, I have adopted it in this book and converted the units used at the time of the tests accordingly. The only other unit which occurs in this text is the roentgen, an outmoded measure of only one type of radiation, gamma rays; it appears in the text simply to demonstrate how the British chose to ignore an important ICRP limit at the tests.

The limits adopted for the British tests were based broadly on recommendations made in 1950 by the ICRP for workers in the nuclear industry. They permitted workers to be exposed to 150 millisieverts a year, three times the limit now in force in the industry.

But the ICRP also suggested a weekly limit for exposure to

gamma rays. British scientists decided to ignore this limit. Instead of limiting exposure to 0.5 roentgens a week, they said it was all right for individuals to be exposed to 3 roentgens at one go – six times the ICRP limit for radiation workers at home. This limit would apply to men who had been given jobs considered essential to the success of the tests, such as retrieving records from contaminated areas after the bomb had exploded. Nine men allotted this task at the Hurricane test got this dose in spite of wearing protective clothing.

The decisions about permitted levels of exposure were taken by Penney and David Barnes, the founder of the health physics branch at the Atomic Weapons Research Department at Aldermaston. During the Royal Commission hearings in London, Peter McClellan, the barrister assisting the commission, asked Barnes if he had known the limits chosen involved a slight risk. 'A very slight risk was regarded as acceptable,' Barnes replied. 'We all thought the doses we were receiving were innocuous.'

By the time the British tests were drawing to a close, in 1958, the ICRP had recognized that its recommended limits were too high. In 1959, it published new limits, the principal change being a reduction in the annual amount of radiation a worker could be exposed to from 150 millisieverts to 50. Effectively, this limit has been in force in the British nuclear industry ever since.

Most of the people who now work in the industry get doses well below the annual limit. The average annual exposure in nuclear power stations like Sizewell A and Dungeness is 5 millisieverts per worker. But at the dirtier end of the industry – the nuclear reprocessing plant at Windscale, in Cumbria – it is nearer 30.

How do these figures compare with the doses received by participants in the British bomb tests? Adam Butler, the junior Defence Minister, has given a detailed breakdown of official records of what the veterans received. It suggests that the vast majority of them were exposed to considerably *less* radiation than people working in the nuclear industry today.

Twenty thousand British servicemen and civilians took part in the tests. Of these, the government says 15,000 were not exposed to radiation. It has records of 6,000 incidents in which the remaining 5,000 men did receive doses of radiation.

The amounts these men got are very low, according to Butler's figures. Fewer than thirty men got a dose higher than 70 millisieverts. These were scientists like James Hole, from AWRE, who got 170 millisieverts when he volunteered to go into the bomb crater soon after the second Mosaic test.

Less than 150 men got between 20 and 70 millisieverts. Five hundred got doses between 3.5 and 20. About 1,500 got less than 3.5 millisieverts. The remaining records of exposure, which show 4,000 occasions on which men were exposed, do not give detailed readings: they establish that exposure took place, but the amount was too small for the equipment used to measure radiation to register it accurately.

The government says exposure at these levels is too small to produce a significant increase in cancer levels. But what is the evidence about the effects of low-level radiation? In fact, the history of radiation protection from the 1950s to the present day has been one in which critics of the nuclear industry have repeatedly argued that the risks of low-level radiation are much greater than the industry admits. Although the controversy has not been resolved, some studies in favour of this hypothesis which were angrily rejected in the 1950s have now won wide acceptance in the scientific community.

Dr Alice Stewart, the epidemiologist who carried out an initial survey of the Christmas Island veterans in 1983, has played a key role in identifying the hazards of low-level radiation. In 1955, as head of the Department of Preventive Medicine at Oxford University, she embarked on a study to find the cause of a sharp rise since the war in the number of children contracting leukaemia.

She discovered that X-rays given to pregnant women were the culprit. She published the results of her work in 1958: it suggested that children whose mothers had had X-rays during pregnancy were *twice as likely* to develop cancer before the age of ten as children whose mothers had not been X-rayed. If the X-ray was given in the first three months of pregnancy, the Oxford study also showed, the child was ten times more likely to develop cancer than if it happened towards the end.

At the time, Stewart's work was challenged. Today, it is so widely accepted that major changes have been made in the use of X-rays during pregnancy. In 1970, Stewart published a follow-up to the Oxford study. It demonstrated a direct relationship between the dose of radiation received by the foetus and the chance of getting cancer. Doubling the number of X-rays also doubled the risk. Significantly, the dose of radiation from an X-ray in the 1960s was only 2 millisieverts.

Alice Stewart's work on the effect of X-rays on the foetus has been complemented by a large-scale study into their effect on adults in the US. In the 1960s, the American scientist, Dr Rosalie Bertell, began work on data from the Tri-State Study, a massive investigation into the health of sixteen million adults in New York State, Maryland and Minnesota. The data included details of each person's life history, including their occupations, where they lived and the illnesses they had suffered.

Before working on the study, Bertell had given little thought to radiation. She had originally trained as a mathematician, but joined a closed order of Carmelite nuns, where she was expected to perform backbreaking physical labour. After an early heart attack, she was advised to join a teaching order, where less physical strength would be required of her. She joined the Grey Nuns of the Sacred Heart and returned to academic work, particularly in the field of the application of maths to medicine and biology. This was exactly the kind of work she was expected to do on the Tri-State Study.

The conclusions she drew from analysis of the data over ten years turned her into a passionate anti-nuclear campaigner. She noticed that the people who suffered from leukaemia were those from wealthy backgrounds with access to private medical care – and X-rays. She also noticed that these people were suffering from a particular sort of leukaemia usually associated with old age very much earlier in life than expected.

Bertell's work, like Stewart's, has brought about changes in the use of X-rays for diagnostic purposes – hospitals in the US use them much more cautiously as a result. But evidence from the effects of X-rays is far from being the only source which suggests low-level radiation is dangerous. In the 1970s, Alice Stewart was asked to go to the US to help analyse the results of a massive study of the health of workers at one of the longest-running nuclear plants in the world – the Hanford works, near Richland, in Washington state.

The Hanford plant was one of the installations set up during the Second World War to carry out work for the Manhattan Project. During the war, its job was to produce plutonium for the bomb; it is now a huge site which houses various types of nuclear reactor, as well as storage tanks for nuclear waste. In 1965, the American nuclear regulatory body, the Atomic Energy Commission, asked Dr Thomas Mancuso, of Pittsburgh University, to look at the health of workers at the Hanford plant.

In 1974, while Mancuso was still working on his study, evidence of a high cancer rate among the Hanford workers was published by Dr Sam Milham, Epidemiology Director of the Washington State Health Department. Milham found there was a higher death rate from certain cancers – cancer of the pancreas, and multiple myeloma, a rare type of bone cancer – among Hanford workers than there was among other industrial employees in the area.

Mancuso's work started to show a similar pattern among the Hanford workers. Suddenly, the US government withdrew his funding and transferred the study elsewhere. Fortunately, Mancuso had kept copies of the data and was able to get funding from the independent Environmental Policy Center in Washington DC. In 1976, he asked Alice Stewart and one of her colleagues at Birmingham University, Dr George Kneale, to help analyse the data. Their initial findings were published in 1977, followed in 1978 by an updated version of the study.

The 1978 report was based on an examination of death certificates for more than 5,000 people who had worked at Hanford over a period of thirty-three years – 1944 to 1977. It found elevated cancer rates among those workers who, according to plant records, had been exposed to radiation. The doses they received were very low – nearly three-quarters had been exposed to less than 20 millisieverts.

Although this study confirmed Milham's earlier work, it provoked a fierce controversy. It is easy to see why. The Hanford study suggested that the ICRP's recommended limit for radiation workers – 50 millisieverts per year – underestimates the risk by at least ten times and possibly as much as thirty times.

This is certainly not the sort of thing the nuclear industry wants to hear, as Dr Rosalie Bertell has pointed out. 'The large number of criticisms of the Hanford worker analysis seems to be related more to its perceived political importance to the foundation of the whole nuclear industry than to its scientific merit.'

Another American study published at the same time as the Hanford findings showed high cancer rates among nuclear workers. Dr Thomas Najarian, of the Boston Veterans Administration Hospital, looked at death certificates for nearly 2,000 workers at the Portsmouth Naval Shipyard, in New Hampshire. He found that their death rate from cancer was twice the national average.

In 1980, yet another significant report was published. It examined the health of more than 3,000 men who participated in an American atom bomb test, code-named Smoky, which took place at the Nevada test site in August 1957. Dr Glyn Caldwell, of the Center for Disease Control in Atlanta, Georgia, reported that the incidence of leukaemia among the men was nearly three times higher than it should have been. Records of exposure were available for eight of the nine men; they all received less than 30 millisieverts. The mean dose for the eight men was only just over 10 millisieverts.

The Smoky test study seemed to provide valuable corroborative evidence of the dangers of low-level radiation, and of the claims of both the American and British veterans. But three years later, Caldwell inexplicably withdrew support from his own study. Dr Rosalie Bertell found herself in the unusual position of defending a study against its author: she considers the Smoky study valid, and says there have been no new findings which necessitate rejection of it.

These studies, and others, suggest the ICRP has consistently underestimated the risk from low-level radiation. A committee set up by the prestigious US National Academy of Science reported on the risk in 1980 and came up with figures that put the risk up to five times higher than the ICRP's estimate. Even then, the committee warned that its own figures 'should in no way be interpreted as precise numerical expectations. They are based on incomplete data and involved a large degree of uncertainty, especially in the low-dose region.'

The committee's own chairman, Professor Edward Radford, of Pittsburgh University, disagreed with its findings. He published a minority report, arguing that the committee was still underestimating the risk. In April 1983, Radford told me he expected a 'cancer epidemic' among nuclear workers unless limits are lowered drastically. They have not been.

Radford came to London in February 1985 to give evidence to the Royal Commission into the British atom bomb tests. He described his research into the health of people in Canonsburg, Pennsylvania, a town still polluted by radioactive waste from its part in the Manhattan Project. During the war, Canonsburg was the site of a factory which processed uranium for the atom bomb; large quantities of radioactive waste are buried beneath the town. The US government has already offered out-of-court settlements to more than thirty residents who claim their health has been affected by radiation.

But Radford's research in Canonsburg threw up one particularly alarming piece of evidence about low-level radiation. 'To my surprise, we found that in Canonsburg there was a significant number of radiation-induced thyroid abnormalities,' he told the Royal Commission. 'I was surprised because the figures said these people had been exposed to radiation in the order of only two or three times natural background.' The thyroid is known to be particularly sensitive to radiation. But the Canonsburg cases appear to have been caused by startlingly low levels of radiation.

In the 1980s, evidence of health problems near nuclear installations in Britain began to mount. Clusters of leukaemia have been reported among people living close to nuclear power stations. One of these is next to the Sizewell A power station, in east Suffolk. A high incidence of leukaemia and cancer of the lymph glands has been noticed among children living near the Oldbury and Berkeley power stations, in the West Country. People living near these plants are exposed to very low levels of radiation.

But the most serious and sustained allegations centre on the reprocessing plant at Windscale, in Cumbria. In November 1983, Yorkshire Television reported high levels of cancer among children in villages near the plant. The government set up an inquiry, under Sir Douglas Black; as it began work, I reported in the *Sunday Times* that doctors were investigating high levels of leukaemia on the west coast of Scotland, right in the path of tides from Windscale. I also reported that doctors in Fleetwood, in Lancashire, to the south of Windscale, had found an unexpectedly high rate of bone-marrow cancer in the area.

When the Black report was published, in July 1984, it proved to be a rather curious document. It confirmed the high incidence of leukaemia in villages near Windscale but shied away from linking it with the plant. Black himself even offered the public a 'qualified reassurance' that the problem had not been caused by Windscale.

The Black report is seriously flawed. First, as James Cutler of Yorkshire Television has shown, it underestimated the cancer rate close to Windscale. Nearly half the cases of childhood cancer in Seascale and nearby villages were left out of the report's analysis. This fact undermines the report's conclusion that the childhood cancer rate in the area is 'unusual but not unparalleled'.

Cutler has also demonstrated that the inquiry miscalculated the dose of radiation received by local children. A meeting held at the DHSS since the publication of the report was told that the inquiry had made an incorrect assumption about the dose to the bone marrow, an error which might mean children living near the plant had got much higher doses of radiation than the Black inquiry assumed.

This error is important; it was the estimate of doses to local children that led the inquiry to rule out radiation as the cause of their cancer. The researchers worked out how many cancers they would expect in the villages if dissident scientists like Alice Stewart were correct about the risk. Because they found *more* cases than this number, they decided radiation could not be the cause. Two other explanations are equally possible: that the inquiry team had underestimated the dose in just the way it now appears they did; or that low-level radiation is more damaging even than critical scientists like Alice Stewart have suggested.

The publication of the Black report has not in any way exonerated Windscale or given a clean bill of health to low doses of radiation. The fact remains that, since the 1950s, a substantial body of evidence has emerged to suggest low-level radiation is very damaging indeed. More and more scientists have added their voices to the growing chorus of concern.

Curiously, one person who seems unaware of these developments is the government's spokesman on the bomb tests, junior Defence Minister Adam Butler. The risks of radiation have been known for years, he said in December 1984, categorically rejecting the suggestion that the British didn't know what they were doing in the 1950s.

'I believe that what I have said ... confirms that the international scientific view of the acceptability of the risks of exposure to ionising radiation has not altered, despite the vastly greater body of data on its effects which has been collected and examined during the period since then,' he announced inexplicably to the House of Commons.

CHAPTER EIGHT

The cloud drifts on

The British government's vehemence in rejecting the allegations of the veterans has been strangely unaffected by the mass of evidence which has emerged since their campaign in the UK started at the end of 1982. Official statements betray not a scintilla of doubt; if anything, the line has become tougher since the questions first began.

Several plausible explanations can be advanced for this state of affairs. One is the traditional reluctance of any current administration to admit faults in its predecessors, even if the events concerned happened thirty years ago and no contemporary ministers are implicated. This convention has a logical, if self-interested origin: each government hopes that its restraint in relation to previous administrations will be emulated by its own successors. It is certainly the case that a degree of loyalty is involved; although the bomb was given the go-ahead by Labour politicians, it was tested in the atmosphere exclusively by Conservatives.

The spectre of numerous compensation claims is another important factor. Although the government is protected by statute from claims for compensation by ex-servicemen for injuries sustained during their period of service, any admission that the tests had led to ill-health would inevitably spark off demands that an exception be made for the men who served at the bomb tests. Since 20,000 men took part, most of them servicemen, such claims could be substantial.

The most powerful motivation to resist the veterans' claims emerges clearly, however, when you look at the direction in which the evidence points. The description of the immediate effects of the bombs given by veterans from various tests –

reddening of the skin resembling sunburn – can be explained by heat and blast from the weapons, particularly at the hydrogen tests, where the energy released was immense. In themselves, these effects tell us little about levels of radiation.

Certain bits and pieces of evidence undoubtedly suggest that men were exposed, on some occasions, to much higher levels of radiation than the government has admitted. Alice Stewart's study of the Christmas Island veterans, published in 1982, contained reports of men suffering from cataracts in middle age. Professor Rotblat pointed out at the time that the occurrence of this disease, usually found only in the elderly, suggested exposure to fairly high levels of radiation.

This situation has an exact parallel in the US. The Defense Nuclear Agency insists American test veterans got only a tenth of the level now permitted annually for radiation workers; Dr Rosalie Bertell says some of the men have symptoms consistent with doses sixty times greater than this amount.

Evidence given to the Australian Royal Commission supports the hypothesis that certain individuals at the British tests – aircrew who flew through atomic clouds, for instance – received fairly high doses of radiation. But if these instances are left to one side, the question remains as to whether large numbers of men could have been exposed to high levels of radiation.

It is clear that some people who appear in official records as receiving no dose of radiation at all nevertheless were exposed – the tasks they were given were mistakenly thought to be safe and they were simply not given monitoring equipment, or it was not collected in. It is also clear that the monitoring equipment used was not as reliable as the British government likes to claim. The evidence is that one of the methods used – film badges – may have underestimated individual doses by 40 per cent.

But there is little evidence to suggest that the doses recorded in official papers are out by a significant degree. What seems more likely is that, with spectacular exceptions, the veterans got doses a little larger than the records suggest but still smaller than those received routinely every year by workers in the nuclear industry.

Once you arrive at this point, it becomes clear that the British government has the strongest possible motive to resist claims by the veterans that radiation has damaged their health. If men exposed to such tiny doses of radiation have suffered elevated rates of disease, what future is there for the nuclear industry, which exposes its workers annually to more radiation than most of the veterans received once in their lifetimes?

The British government must now fear that Conservative ministers did more in the 1950s than explode a series of nuclear weapons in Australia and the Pacific. They may have unintentionally planted a time-bomb under every nuclear power station in Britain.

If the government was committed to a searching and unimpeachably independent study into the veterans' claims about the bomb tests, it chose a curious way of going about it. Instead of selecting a university department to carry out the study, it gave the job to a body with close links to the nuclear industry. It was a peculiar choice for a study whose results could, in the end, do untold damage to that industry.

As if that in itself was not bad enough, the study is too narrow in scope; the largest of the organizations representing the British veterans, the British Nuclear Tests Veterans' Association, has dissociated itself from the study and says it has no confidence in its eventual results.

The government announced its intention to commission the study in January 1983. Its motives were far from altruistic. The veterans' complaints had just been aired in a blaze of publicity in newspapers and on television and the announcement could be interpreted as an attempt by the government to silence the subject by taking action which could not possibly produce results for a matter of years. Having made the announcement, the government took nearly eight months to award the contract.

When it did, it took the surprising step of giving it to the National Radiological Protection Board (NRPB). This body, set up by Act of Parliament in 1970, acts as watchdog on Britain's nuclear industry. Unfortunately, its independence is seriously undermined by its close links with that industry; and its structure and history suggest it suffers from much the same problems as the International Commission on Radiological Protection. Its staff tend to be people who have previously worked for the nuclear industry, and it has taken positions in the past that will not hinder nuclear power.

This very problem was spotted in 1977 by Sir Brian Flowers, who chaired the Royal Commission on Environmental Pollution. He pointed out that many of the NRPB's staff had previously worked for the body which oversees the development of nuclear energy, the United Kingdom Atomic Energy Authority, and the two organizations are based at the same rather remote place, Harwell.

'In making these remarks we intend in no way to impugn the integrity of the present members or staff of the Board,' Flowers said, 'but rather to emphasize the importance of fostering not only the reality, but the appearance, of independence.' His recommendations – reconstruction at board level and a review of the organization and expertise of the expert body – have never been carried out.

The links with the nuclear industry affect the organization's top level including its director. From 1971 to 1981, the job was done by Dr A. S. McLean, who was also, for the greater part of his time as NRPB director, a member of the ICRP. Before his appointment at NRPB, he held three different positions with the United Kingdom Atomic Energy Authority.

This tradition continued with the appointment in 1982 of McLean's successor, John Dunster. Dunster appeared in chapter 7 as one of the longest-serving members of the ICRP and its committees; in the days before the UKAEA was set up, Dunster worked for the Ministry of Supply nuclear plants at Harwell and Windscale. He later held senior positions in the UKAEA.

In 1958, while working for the UKAEA's health and safety branch, Dunster went to a UN conference on the peaceful uses of atomic energy, where he provided an illuminating insight into what was happening at Windscale. Discharges from the plant, he said, were part of a deliberate experiment to find out more about the movement of radioactive substances in the environment. Although these discharges were not considered dangerous at the time by the scientists responsible for them, they are now under suspicion of being the cause of leukaemia near the plant.

The NRPB's own record does not suggest it is a speedy and vigilant protector of the public when it comes to radiation. Although it was set up in 1970, the NRPB did not produce a report into Britain's worst nuclear accident, the fire at Windscale in 1957, until 1983. That report was produced only after an independent environmental research organization, the Political Ecology Research Group, came up with its own report in 1981, suggesting that numerous cases of thyroid cancer could have been caused by the fire.

When the NRPB's own report on the fire appeared, one oversight quickly became clear. The NRPB report included estimates of the number of cancers likely to have been caused in the population of the UK by the radioactive substances released by the fire, but failed to consider one of the most carcinogenic, the isotope called polonium 210. After I pointed out in the *Sunday Times* that polonium 210 had come out of the pile during the fire, the NRPB was forced to issue an addendum to its report, increasing its estimate of the number of cancers probably caused by the fire. What made the omission of polonium 210 from the first report even odder was that traces of it were found near the plant immediately after the fire by John Dunster, then a health physicist and, by the time of the report, the NRPB's director.

But it was not only the choice of the NRPB to carry out the study of the veterans that sat oddly with the claim that it was to be an independent survey. The scientists originally chosen to do the work at NRPB included Dr John Reissland, a public critic of Alice Stewart's work on low-level radiation. In 1978, Reissland published an assessment of the Hanford study – the important study of nuclear workers in the US published by Stewart with Thomas Mancuso and George Kneale – which dismissed most of their conclusions. 'There is wide agreement that the Hanford study ... does not represent a valid statistical interpretation of the actual data,' he wrote. Reissland's conclusion is disingenuous: it would be nearer the truth to say that the Hanford study is controversial, with no general agreement on its conclusions. The choice of Reissland to look into the veterans' claims looked at the very least combative, given that their cause was first championed by Alice Stewart.

After the study was set up, Reissland's death in a fire at his home necessitated a change in the team carrying out the work. This event, and other problems, means that the study will be published later than planned – at the time of writing, it is unlikely to appear before late 1986.

The veterans themselves are highly critical of the study. It will look at only two issues: whether there is a higher death rate among the veterans than in a comparable group of servicemen who did not take part in the tests, and whether more of the veterans have contracted cancer than men in the comparable group.

Several problems are immediately obvious. First, there is to be no attempt to contact individuals. This means that the researchers will rely on death certificates for the cause of death, yet some cancers are well known to be under-reported as a cause of death. This method could lead to cancers being missed.

Second, the study is confined to looking at only one disease – cancer. It is impossible to differentiate between cancer caused by radiation and cancer caused by some other agent. But the study has excluded an examination of the incidence of cataract – a disease which can be caused by radiation – among the veterans. This condition, which usually occurs only in the elderly, would be a significant indicator of radiation-related problems if it was found to have occurred among the veterans, most of whom are only in their middle years.

Third, the study will not look at genetic effects. A number of men who took part in the tests have reported deformity or illness among their children. This is a difficult area: although scientists have no doubt radiation can cause genetic effects, they have not yet observed them in an irradiated population. But if studies on people who have been exposed to radiation exclude consideration of genetic effects, that situation will never change. The NRPB study ignores the opportunity to look for genetic effects among the veterans.

All in all, the veterans believe the study is being carried out by the wrong organization and with the wrong terms of reference. They also think it is a way of stalling their claims: the government has made it clear it will not change its position until the NRPB has reported. At the moment, that report is not due to appear until nearly *four years* after the British veterans first aired their complaints in public.

Frank Cook, the Labour MP for Stockton North, summed up the feelings of many veterans when he spoke in a debate on the tests in the House of Commons in December 1984. Cook expressed his disappointment that the NRPB had nothing to report by then.

Instead of commissioning a statistical survey, the British government should have set up a Royal Commission into the tests, he said. 'Ultimately, the people who were in the front line will die out the longer this goes on,' he said. 'We have a responsibility not only to them but to the generations after them.'

As well as a proper investigation into what happened at the tests, many of the veterans also want compensation. Men who have suffered chronic illnesses, and the wives and children of men who have died, feel the least the British government can do is give them cash payments or pensions. So far, their attempts to prise money from the government have achieved minimal success.

The major obstacle is the Crown Proceedings Act 1947. Section 10 bars servicemen from bringing claims for compensation against the government for injuries received during their period of service. The thinking behind it is obvious: the government simply could not cope if every serviceman injured during a war was subsequently entitled to demand large amounts of cash from the state. But the veterans say their case is different – that what happened to them had not been envisaged by the people who drafted the Act. The government has shown no sympathy towards this line of argument.

The veterans are in the process of mounting a court challenge to the Act and they are also preparing cases on behalf of civilians who took part in the tests and who are not covered by the prohibition in the Act. Such actions are inevitably costly, and the British Nuclear Tests Veterans' Association is still trying to raise money to pay for them.

In the meantime, they are trying to devise other ways to gain official recognition that they have been affected by radiation. Open verdicts have been recorded at inquests on a handful of veterans who have died of diseases that could be linked with radiation, but the most important attempt to use an inquest as a forum for the men's claims proved unsuccessful.

In April 1985, an inquest jury returned a verdict of natural causes on the death of Kenneth Measures, a former chief petty officer in the navy, who suffered a rare form of lung cancer after taking part in the first British hydrogen bomb test at Malden Island in 1957. The veterans had hoped for a verdict of unlawful killing.

Coroners' courts have come in for much criticism in recent years and, in retrospect, it seems a little optimistic of the veterans to believe that inquests might provide a useful alternative route to justice. But the veterans have scored one major success elsewhere, with a ruling at a pensions tribunal which does appear to undermine the government's insistence that absolutely no one has been harmed by radiation.

Mick Saffrey, an RAF radio operator who spent several months at Christmas Island after the 1958 tests, applied to the DHSS for a war pension in 1980 on the grounds that he had suffered cataracts and gone blind as a result of radiation. When his application was turned down, he appealed. On 26 July 1984, a DHSS pensions tribunal ruled that he should receive compensation. The form of the award – whether it will be a pension or a lump sum – has not been decided at the time of writing.

Saffrey's eyesight has been partially restored after an operation. He also suffers from a low sperm count, which could be attributable to radiation. The pensions tribunal ruled that even if it ignored the evidence of the sperm count, 'we feel that we are left unsure that the cataracts were not caused by Christmas Island radiation. It follows from this that the appeal must be allowed, on the basis that the disability is attributable to service.'

After the successful appeal Saffrey said that he was convinced his condition had been caused by radiation. 'These things were exploded over the water and we used the same water to wash in,' he said. 'I never once saw a sign on Christmas Island saying you couldn't go anywhere. We used to wander all over the place, as we had nothing else to do.'

The Ministry of Defence denies that the Saffrey case makes any difference at all to its claim that no one has been injured by the tests. The tribunal had not ruled that radiation *caused* his condition, a spokesman told me, only that it *might* have done. Nevertheless, the British Nuclear Tests Veterans' Association believes the case is the first chink in the government's armour and intends to go on fighting on as many fronts as possible for the compensation it believes should be paid to many of its 1,300 members.

That the wind of change is blowing in their direction is in little doubt. Already, the Canadian government has earmarked the equivalent of £17 million to pay compensation to veterans who took part in nuclear tests – Canada did not mount atom bomb tests but its servicemen were present at those staged by other countries, just as the Australians were.

There is one more thing that many of the veterans want, and that is an end to the testing of nuclear weapons. Their concern is a timely reminder that Britain's final test in the atmosphere, on 23 September 1958, did not mark the end but only a change in Britain's weapons-testing programme.

With an atmospheric test ban treaty a near certainty in the foreseeable future, the nuclear powers were already looking for alternative ways of testing bombs. The obvious place to put the tests was underground. Britain's thoughts inevitably turned to its accommodating ally, Australia; for a time, the British were scouting round for a suitable Australian mountain in which they could drill a hole and blow up a bomb.

Fortunately for Australia, the plan came to nothing. The first joint British and American bomb test took place at the Nevada test site in the US on 1 March 1962. The test, code-named Pampas, took place 1,200 feet underground. Immediately after the explosion, two small clouds escaped from the ground and floated away.

Leaks of this sort from underground tests in Nevada have become a regular occurrence. Inhabitants of Cedar City, Utah, who live downwind from the Nevada test site, have formed an organization to campaign for an end to nuclear tests; they say forty-three underground tests have leaked radiation, endangering communities close to the site.

In fact, there have been far more nuclear tests since the Partial Test Ban Treaty was signed in 1963 than took place before it. By June 1976, official figures show that the US alone had tested a staggering 588 nuclear weapons; only 183 of these were detonated in the atmosphere before the signing of the treaty.

During the 1970s, the US actually stepped up its testing programme. The figures rose from around eight underground nuclear tests in 1972 to sixteen in 1975. Russian tests recently declined in number; they went down from twenty in 1978 to four in 1982.

Britain's nuclear test programme has never been in the same league as that of Russia or the US. But it has carried steadily on: one Anglo–American test in Nevada in 1979, three in 1980. Details are scant; the joint test carried out at Nevada on 25 April 1982 was between 20 and 150 kilotons, the official American statement announced uninformatively.

Nuclear testing is not an episode in our past, as peculiar to the 1950s as the beatniks and James Dean. Britain is, on paper, committed to working towards a complete test ban treaty. In fact, since they started in 1977, the talks have been bogged down in arguments over how to ensure the other side is not breaking the treaty.

In 1939, when the splitting of the atom coincided with the outbreak of the Second World War, the scientific world was infected with the contagion of secrecy. That development, which flew in the face of a long tradition of sharing information about scientific discoveries, concentrated the fruits of an international and rather haphazard quest for knowledge in the hands of one country, the US, which tried to exploit its position of superior knowledge for its own gain.

America's shortsighted attempt to gain advantage through its almost accidental possession of the bomb produced the atmosphere of distrust which led to the arms race. An agreement to end nuclear tests, because it would require a degree of trust between the signatories, would be a first step towards reversing the baleful situation which has existed since the Second World War. That such a step has not been taken is a measure of how little the contagion of secrecy and distrust has loosened its grip in the forty years since it first took hold.

BIBLIOGRAPHY

Bertell, Rosalie. *No Immediate Danger*. The Women's Press, 1985

Bertin, Leonard. *Atom Harvest*. Secker and Warburg, 1955

Eden, Anthony. *Full Circle* (memoirs). Cassell, 1960

Glasstone, S. *The Effects of Nuclear Weapons*. United States Atomic Energy Commission, 1957

Gowing, Margaret. *Britain and Atomic Energy, 1939–1945*. Macmillan, 1964

  Independence and Deterrence: Britain and Atomic Energy, 1945–1952. Volume I, *Policy Making*. Volume II, *Policy Execution*. Macmillan, 1974

Ground Zero Organization. *Nuclear War – What's In It for You*. Methuen, 1982

Gyorgy, Anna, and friends. *No Nukes*. South End Press, Boston, 1979

Harris, Kenneth. *Attlee*. Weidenfeld and Nicolson, 1982

Heckstall-Smith, H. W. *Atomic Radiation Dangers and What They Mean to You*. J. M. Dent and Sons, 1958

Jungk, Robert. *Brighter Than A Thousand Suns*. Penguin, 1964

Kimball Smith, Alice, and Weiner, Charles (eds.). *Robert Oppenheimer, Letters and Recollections*. Harvard University Press, 1980

Kunetka, James W. *Oppenheimer: The Years of Risk*. Prentice-Hall, New Jersey, 1982

Macmillan, Harold. *Tides of Fortune, 1945–1955*. Macmillan, 1969

Mazuzan, George T., and Walker, J. Samuel. *Controlling the Atom: The Beginnings of Nuclear Regulation, 1946–1962*. University of California Press, n.d.

Menaul, Stewart. *Countdown: Britain's Strategic Nuclear Forces*. Robert Hale, 1980

Pauling, Linus. *No More War!* Victor Gollancz, 1958

Pincher, Chapman, BSc. *Into the Atomic Age*. Hutchinson, 1948

Pochin, Edward. *Nuclear Radiation: risks and benefits*. Clarendon Press, 1983

Pringle, Peter, and Spigelman, James. *The Nuclear Barons*. Michael Joseph, 1981

Rosenberg, Howard L. *Atomic Soldiers: American Victims of Nuclear Experiments*. Beacon Press, Boston, 1980

Bibliography

Saffer, Thomas H., and Kelly, Orville E. *Countdown Zero*. G. P. Putnam's Sons, New York, 1982

Sternglass, Ernest. *Secret Fallout: Low-Level Radiation from Hiroshima to Three-Mile Island*. McGraw-Hill, 1981

Stockholm International Peace Research Institute. *Nuclear Radiation in Warfare*. Taylor and Francis, 1981

Tame, Adrian, and Robotham, F. P. J. Maralinga – British A-Bomb Australian Legacy. Fontana Books, Melbourne, 1982

INDEX